EVERY
NEED TO KNOW
I LEARNED IN
BOY SCOUTS

EVERYTHING I NEED TO KNOW I LEARNED IN BOY SCOUTS

THE STORY OF TROOP 826

RICHARD J. BENNETT

ISBN on back cover, 3rd Edition

Illustrated by the Author

For the Troop

Summer Camp, Camp Texoma, August 1967

CONTENTS

FOREWORD

MY BROTHER KEVIN AND I grew up in Irving, Texas in the 1960s. The Bennett family lived just down the street and around the corner. With a younger and older brother, the Bennett family was a perfect match for my family, and we became great friends and playmates. Although we didn't know it at the time, we were living some of the best years of our lives. From fireflies to Frankenstein, it was our magic time, our "wonder years." It's sad how some of the simplest pleasures and sweetest memories can be so easily forgotten. Lucky for me, Richard managed to retain his in detail. Forty-plus years later, after I lost my brother Kevin in a tragic accident, Richard brought those memories out and gave them to me as a gift in the form of a small book. It's a marvelous treat, to relive your childhood through someone else's perspective and relish the little gems that their mind's eye summons from the past. It was a gift I cherish to this day.

I recommended to Richard that he continue writing, and this book is the result. The following pages are a recollection of another magic time, our time as Scouts. It meant countless things to each of us. It was a coming of age, growing from childhood to adolescence, learning responsibility, forging lifetime friendships, and discovering who we were. Through the years, for every young man who wore the red and white embroidered numbers of 826, Scoutmaster Warren Street was there. He was the keel. He was the heart. He was our inspiration. Other than my father, never have I met a man that I loved and respected more.

Aldous Huxley said, "Every man's memory is his private literature."

So, reader, venture in and share these memories and perhaps awaken some reminiscent of a time in your own life.

Mike Quine
June 6, 2009

ACKNOWLEDGEMENTS

I NEED TO EXPRESS MY appreciation to the following for their help in putting this story together.

First, in my immediate family, thanks to my parents, Raymond and Marjorie Bennett, who supported and drove us to the Scout meetings each week, who purchased our Scout uniforms and equipment, and who had hopes for us. To my big brother David, for being the person I followed and tried to copy. To my sister Kathy, who organized all of the stories on the computer when this task got too big for me to handle alone.

To David Couric, who read and edited this text before submission to the publishers. To Jan Hart and Kevin Kendro, Irving Public Library Archivists, who helped me dig up facts concerning Old Irving, the Estelle Community, and George Alford.

In the Scouting Group, thanks to Mr. Warren Street, Scoutmaster, for being the leader once again and for my first interview. To Ray Mahaffey Sr. and Lois Mahaffey, parents of Eagle Scout Ray Mahaffey Jr., for their time and viewpoints. To Mike Quine, who gave me the inspiration and motivation for this book. To Duane Tarver, Jack Rankin, Steve Rackley, Mark Dixon, Mike Huebner, Chuck Wagner, and Jerry Thetford, first of all for their friendship and then for their interviews and encouragement.

Thanks to Eagle Scouts H.M. "Smoky" Eggers and Jeff Goodgame, for pointing me in the direction of an editor and correcting any scouting technical terms.

Finally, thanks to the Circle 10 Council and the Boy Scouts of America for the great memories. I have loved the Boy Scouts in a way that is almost comparable to loving the people of Church. Whenever we Scouts run into each other as adults now, we laugh as we recall our colorful and formative past, saying, "Remember when ...?"

INTRODUCTION

I NEED TO LET THE READER know that I never finished my Boy Scout journey. I was like most, those who joined purely for the fun of it and who never really caught on to the concept of responsibility and hard work until later years. I made it to the rank of Star, and then I was overcome by other factors in life . . . school, work, lack of time, lack of energy, adolescence, and other excuses. It wasn't until many years later that I realized how much Scouting contributed to my having a wholesome and fun experience during my growing up time. This was not something shared by most young men.

This is the story of a troop located in the north Texas area, in the city of Irving. It lasted only about 15 years, with over 200 boys experiencing more or less the same things I did while affiliated with Troop 826, led for a dozen years by Scoutmaster Warren Street.

Mr. Street was so much a part of the troop that it's impossible to think of Scouting days without thinking of him. I considered using the title "Scoutmaster" for this book, but since it's a history of the troop and not a biography, the other title took precedence.

I still carry a little guilt over not having finished my scouting years on the high note of the Eagle badge. It's followed me all through the years. I considered my shortcoming in that area when trying to decide whether or not to stay more years with the Air Force Reserves . . . I stayed a total of 23 years. I wanted to get that last stripe and become a Chief Master Sergeant. I didn't want to repeat what I had done with the Boy Scouts, which was to quit too early. Only later did I come to peace with the decision that I wasn't really quitting, only retiring. I also realized that with the government, sometimes circumstances can work against you when it comes to making rank, whereas in the Scouts, it's up to the Scout himself as to how far he can go.

I wanted to put this history together to thank Mr. Street for his many years of leadership with us boys. We all feel the same way, I'm sure. I also wanted to put this together for the boys in the troop.

I felt it needed to be written. This is not the whole story, just the viewpoint of one Scout.

I also hope that any present and future Scouts who happen to read this will learn to have fun and make the most of their Scouting experience.

Update

It's been ten years since I first wrote 'Everything I Need …', and this is the third edition to see daylight. The book has been moved from Landmark Press and is now self-published through Createspace in Amazon. It was once criticized in a review as not being what Scouting was all about; I guided the reviewer to the sub-title, plainly seen on the cover; explaining that this is not about the total program, this is the account of one local troop, Troop 826.

Sadly, fellow scouts have since passed away, including Richard Salas, who I knew as a younger scout, a good person with a fun personality, also brother to Jack Rankin, one of our Troop's Eagle Scouts. We also lost Steve Rackley, another Eagle Scout, and close friend to Chuck Wagner. Steve stayed active with the scouting programs through Order of the Arrow, and had three sons to earn the Eagle badge.

Mr. Street is well into his mid-90s and still independent as ever; however, Mrs. Street (Lura) passed away about a year ago. Mr. Mahaffey is also into his mid-90s and remembers all the good times, but Mrs. Mahaffey has also passed away.

The first edition often referred to an 826 website, created by Eagle Scout Michael Quine. He did this out of love for the troop, and it was up for a few years before it was suddenly removed by the internet provider. Perhaps it will reappear again one day, in a safer, more secure website.

This was my first attempt at putting a book together, and so far is my best seller. People seem to enjoy reading about the Scouting program, even though much of this account took place over fifty years ago and tells the story of only one troop.

CHAPTER ONE

RESPONSIBILITY VERSUS FUN

T HERE WAS ALWAYS A TIME during the Thursday night Scout meetings I dreaded, and that was when one of the leaders would speak on the subject of making rank or earning merit badges. After you become a First Class Scout, if you're going to progress to the next level, you have to earn merit badges. This idea was always a stress point for me. I felt as though someone had a tight grip on my stomach as soon as the subject was brought up. Envisioning the merit badge tasks ahead, I knew I couldn't do it all. Like my big brother David said, I should have focused on the little tasks instead of the whole picture.

I would get that feeling, just like in church, when the preacher would talk about how we were supposed to go out and witness to the unchurched. I used to wonder why the unchurched couldn't get themselves up and out of bed and go to church like anyone else in a free society. There's a church on every block. What's keeping them from getting there? Why should I be involved? I felt that religion was fairly personal; I didn't know how to talk to others about it without sounding like a salesman. It was the kind of feeling I would get whenever I saw a textbook with small print. I read only what was inviting, whatever I was interested in. If the print wasn't big enough to suit my tastes, then I would find something else to read, like maybe a comic book! In the merit badge booklets, there was plenty of small print; small print represented boredom to this Scout. I didn't want to concentrate on specifics; I wanted to have fun with generalities!

I went to the Scout meetings to have fun, to be with the guys, to play games, and to go camping. I didn't go to the meetings to be reminded what a poor scholar I was. I was already well aware of that fact. Goals and responsibility hadn't yet sunk in for me. My desire to learn didn't kick in until I was far away from the public school system, and by that time, it was almost too late for me to do much learning or lay any solid educational groundwork for myself.

If you can face small print without fear, then you can go far in the Scouting program. Learn what you can; earn what you can. Get a magnifying glass if you have to; it'll make the print bigger.

In an interview with Eagle Scout Jack Rankin, he told me that he wished he hadn't been so intense when he was young. He wished he had concentrated on having a little more fun. I told him if he hadn't been so intense he might not have gone as far as he did. I wish I had concentrated on having fun a little less and accepted my responsibilities. I wish I had faced the academic challenges of the Scouting program. I might have gone further, like Jack.

When I talked to my brother David about what he thought he came away with concerning Scouting, he said:

"Well, I think more than anything, it kind of gave me the confidence that I could do more than I thought I could do . . . maybe I learned some coping mechanisms—be prepared, work hard, be where you're supposed to be when you're supposed to be there, and then when you're not prepared, look around and see what's available for you to use . . . Boy Scouts, it was really my first leadership responsibility, being Patrol Leader. I was leader of the Eagle Patrol for a while. So that was my first opportunity to act in a leadership role of any type. So I guess I really gained that, more than anything, confidence in myself and also that I could work with others and lead them."

Responsibility is a slippery concept, and just when you think you've got it, it may slip away again. Fun, on the other hand, is an easy to understand. If you can find a workable balance between the two, chances are good that you will be a well-rounded individual, a well-rounded Scout. Learning can be turned into fun; it doesn't have to be a chore.

CHAPTER TWO

RITES OF PASSAGE: PRANKS

The Geek

W HEN YOUNG SCOUTS ARE AWAY from their structured home environment, there's something about the freedom that leads to experimentation. One means of experimentation is the prank, usually pulled by the older Scout on younger, unsuspecting ones. If the younger Scouts are on guard, then the older Scout may look for other game, say, members of another troop. Scouts could be secretive when freedom and fun was at stake. Pranks, if done right, could result in a story that could be told for years.

The older Scouts didn't really consider the consequences of their actions; they were only concerned with the thrill of planning and executing the stunts. There was some risk involved, but somehow this was overlooked. It just didn't figure into anybody's plans.

One weekend, when my brother David was still active with the troop, we all went camping at Possum Kingdom. At this particular campout, Mark Dixon and Jack Rankin, two of the older Scouts, brought along something that not many Scouts had access to: a full-sized rubber mask that would fit down over a grown adult's head.

Where did Jack get the money for a mask like that? When I was growing up, I rarely had 15¢ in my pocket and had to depend on an allowance and mowing lawns for extra money—for any money! Even when we managed to get a few bucks, our parents always encouraged us to put it in the bank, for the future, for college. Jack's mask would have cost around $15 in the 1960s, which was a lot of money to an adolescent boy. If our parents saw us spending our lawn-mowing earnings on items like that, well, they would have been angry. We'd have felt a little guilty if we had bought something like that. Since guilt never interfered with my foolish spending habits, I felt guilty a lot growing up.

The mask was huge, made of rubber, and flexible. It was lightweight and comfortable, not too much of a burden to wear. It was shaped into the ugliest face you could imagine, like Quasimodo, the Hunchback of Notre Dame. Its huge lips were open, showing uneven teeth and a large tongue; the hair was a mess; the eyes were so big they were almost out of their sockets, and they were uneven—one eye looked one direction, while the other eye looked another; and the nose was flat and misshapen. Put this all together and you've got one huge headed, ugly man.

My brother David was a big kid who liked to have fun, and he was powerfully built. On the field, at times he was like the Juggernaut; once he gained momentum, there was no force on earth that could stop him. When playing backyard football, I had learned not to tackle him from the front but only to trip him up from the side or back. It was safer that way.

The mask and David were made for each other. Putting the two together on a camping trip, they became "The Geek."

There's just something about scaring somebody that became a game in our troop. Wandering off into other campsites to scare Scouts of other troops became known as 'raids.' It was one thing to scare people you knew, but that soon wore thin. Scaring people you *didn't* know, now that was sport! So on Saturday night, the last night of the campout, off David went on his mission: to scare the tar out of unknown Scouts.

David was out that night in another campsite. Those Scouts were already in their tents, as we were at our campsite, so

David was really breaking two unwritten Scout rules: Don't leave your campsite after *Taps,* and don't wander into anyone else's campsite after lights out. Yet, the mission needed accomplishing.

The Geek (aka David Bennett)

David found a lone tent. Since one troop's patrols would usually be away from the other troop's patrols, the tent made easy prey. David looked around, pulled the rubber mask out of his shirt, and placed it over his head. He poked his head into the tent of the unsuspecting Scouts. What he heard was "What's that?" Evidently it was dark. "I don't know." "Get your flashlight." (Click) David yells. Kids scream. David sees kids fall out of their cots. David runs. It's a good thing he runs, because one Scout has enough presence of mind to fight the night beast. This Scout grabbed a broom and charged David, swinging it at him like a baseball bat. Fortunately, David had been exercising all summer with the Irving swim team and was able to elude his pursuer. He would have been quicker in his getaway, but the rubber eyeholes were difficult to see through, something he hadn't counted on.

I don't know how many tents he surprised that night, but I don't think there were too many. Running for your life can make you count the cost of frightening others. It boiled down to the question: Was it worth it? Hearing the screams of strange Scouts as they faced their imagined demise? Yeah, it was worth it.

David remembers this prank fondly:

"Jack Rankin had somehow gotten a hold of this mask that was just—it was a scary mask. The guy looked like Quasimodo. It was a rubber mask, basically, but it was a well-done rubber mask. It wasn't one of those little cheapie Ben Franklin five-and-dime store masks you see for Halloween. It was a dadgum over-the-head mask, soft rubber, had eyeholes, nose holes, even a place to stick your tongue out if you wanted to; don't know why anybody would want to do that. The eyes were all misshapen; the face was distorted; it looked like it was melted and sliding, just horrible, horrible. Looked kind of like my brother-in-law. (Laughs) I'm kidding here. They had taken that to camp with us, to Camp Possum Kingdom, I think; yeah, it was! That was the year you and I had been on the swim team with the Irving Swim League. I had lost some weight, so I was lean and mean, skinny, and still had hair. The thing was, the older Scouts, Jack and I think Mark Dixon, used to like to go around and scare the younger campers in our camp; and then, well, it was just a natural progression; we had to branch out, of course, and go visit the other troops! I mean, you can only scare the same guys so many times! We had to expand, you see, so we went out there. Well, I didn't go out with any particular guys. I know that Mark and Jack had talked about it, and I said, "You know, I think I'm going to do that!" And so I took the mask, and I went out and we went over to a campsite where another troop was, and you know they had tents, three boys per tent, and they were on wooden platforms, so they were a lot nicer than what we carried with us to go on our campouts. They were permanent tents, so to speak. It was maybe 9:30 to 10:30 at night, not too terribly late. I heard some guys talking in this tent; they were kind of off by themselves in one corner of the camp. It seems they probably had 20 or 30 feet between each tent. Maybe you'd have two of them clustered together. Anyway, there was this one place with two tents; I didn't bother with what Jack and Mark would do, they'd go out there and kind of make some noises out there in the bushes, rattle some bushes around, start growling a little bit, then they'd jump into the tent. Man, I just went full frontal; I just jumped on in there and "RAARRRRRGGHHRRR!!" These kids were kind of between boyhood and being teenagers, sitting around talking about goofy stuff like whether Mighty Mouse could beat up Superman, and then you'd talk about girls, then you'd go back to talk about Mighty Mouse and Superman. So we were at that funny age there, so most of the kids just screamed like girls. I remember one guy fell out of his cot and actually fell onto the ground; and another guy, though, there was one young man who took action; I mean, by gosh, he was scared but he was brave, and he grabbed up a broomstick and started coming after me, and I knew that I had probably overstayed my welcome, so I started running. Thank goodness I had lost that weight that summer and was in pretty good shape; I was able to outrun that guy, but I was having a hard time making my way out because that stupid mask was over my head, and I was unable to see out of the eye holes, and I wore glasses even back then, and they had turned all sideways underneath the mask, and I was trying to run down a dark road that was not paved. It was a gravel road, and the kid who was chasing me tripped and fell down, and of course being the good Scout that I was, I left him there. I didn't go back and help him, but I didn't go back and kick him while he was down, either!"

When Mr. Street found out about David's escapades, he, as David put it, "got ripped pretty good." You didn't want to get chewed out by Mr. Street. He was usually right. What's worse, he usually sounded right, which could make you feel pretty small for whatever it was you did. After getting set straight, you didn't fall back into whatever it was you were into that made him so mad. You had to find a new type of deviancy to explore.

Mark Dixon had a similar episode as "The Geek" where some of his pranks didn't exactly work out as planned, and he discovered that sometimes a good scare could backfire:

"I think it was at Camp Wisdom. It was summer camp. A bunch of us were in camp together and Jack Rankin was the one who brought the mask. He had an uncle or somebody who gave him this professional-looking mask; I mean it was weird and wicked. Somehow or other I decided I was going to put it on, and we decided we were going to go out and see how many kids we could scare. My memory of it is getting in front of a tent; everybody was behind me; they were all going, "Go after them!" I got in front of this tent, and kids were asleep, and as I was standing in front of the tent, I'd growl "R-r-r-r!" and they'd kind of start waking up, and I'd growl again. About the third time I did it, flashlights started flipping on, going everywhere, and I went running out of the campsite, and we all stood over in the bushes giggling and laughing until I don't know how long, until the lights finally went back down, the flashlights went off, and it seemed like things started settling back down. Unfortunately, I decided to go back for an encore. I got in front of the tent; I did my little thing again, making noises; nothing happened. I did it again; nothing happened. About the third time I did it, I got the wicked feeling that I was being watched. And so I started walking, then running, and running at full speed trying to get out of the campsite, and the next thing I knew, I had three or four guys on top of me beating the daylights out of me . . . and a couple of my guys came running around the corner to rescue me, and I remember having a standoff with them. There wasn't any fighting going on between them, but they kept telling me they were going to cut my hair because I had a little bit longer hair back then.

I was glad all my guys showed up; there were like four of our guys, and there was, I don't know, a whole camp full of other guys. Somehow they got me out of there, and I thought we were going to be in really big trouble the next morning. I think the rest of the staff, what have you, at the campsite got wind of it. They kind of gave me a little bit of grief the next day, but everybody knew it was just in fun, and it finally blew over a little bit."

Wild Man

Mark didn't quite stop at tricks with masks for fun around the camp; as he remembered, there were a few more tricks to be played, again at another tour of Camp Wisdom where the higher-ranking Scouts had been preparing the minds of the newer Scouts with the tale of a Wild Man last seen roaming loose at night on the grounds. According to Mark:

"Some of us older Scouts got together and decided to take a bunch of the young guys to the showers one night. We devised this thing. I believe Mark Null was going to be the one that we'd get him down in the bottom of a ravine, a dried creek bed that had like 10-foot-high steep banks on each side, just covered with trees. So it was really dark at 8:30 or 9 p.m. at night. It was pretty dark to be taking a bunch of kids to the showers, leading them over there. So all of us had our towels, soap, shampoo, whatever; and Null, we had him strategically placed down at the bottom of the ravine with ketchup poured all over him. Mike Quine played the Wild Man. He had a machete or something. So as the kids came down, and we all had flashlights, like I say it was dark, the flashlights flipped over to where you could see Null laying there with ketchup all over him. The next thing you saw as the kids flipped their flashlights up, there was Quine with a machete or something standing there, and I mean scared the daylights. The kids went climbing the hills trying to get out of that ravine. I mean climbing over each other to get away; it was priceless. Well, you know, I was prepared for it all because I had been in on the planning part of it, but when I saw everything transpire, it scared the daylights out of *me!*"

Radiation Man

Toward the end of his Scoutmaster career, I believe Mr. Street had figured out that it was hard to keep kids from pulling jokes on each other, especially after they had found their new form of freedom on campouts. So he decided that if anyone was going to be the prankster on a mass scale, it was going to be him and the staff. This way he could keep control of the troop, keep the kids from wandering off into other camps, and make sure that nobody got hurt.

Chuck Wagner recalls the days of "Radiation Man." He had been working on his Camping merit badge and had to separate himself from the rest of the troop to sleep in his previously prepared shelter, this after hearing the tales at the campfire of a local man driven insane from radiation poisoning:

"Oh yeah, Mr. Street and Mr. Johnson were real good about coming up with stories and getting into character. Mr. Street would tell the story, and Mr. Calvin Johnson would be out in the woods making a ruckus. What they did back then, they would take this glow stick; you know, you break it, and it has a fluorescent glow, this green fluorescent glow . . . well, back then, we'd never seen one. We didn't know what it was. It was still fairly new then. What they'd do, they'd break that; usually they'd wear a white T-shirt, and they'd break that thing, and they'd tie a string around it, and they'd tie it around their neck, and put it underneath their white T-shirt so you'd see something glowing from their chest. Mr. Street would usually get, uh, I guess they use them for tanning salons, the little goggles, they look like big white eyes, and there are little pupils in them that you can see through, I think they're like sunglass shade lenses, very small pupils, so you have these big bug eyes, and then Mr. Street would finish it off . . . by sticking his chompers out. He's worn dentures for as long as we've known him. He would stick those chompers out of his mouth halfway out, and he'd come at you like Young Frankenstein with the glow stick and the big bug eyes. You didn't know what was going on, and of course he'd be wrapped up in something or other so you couldn't quite tell who it was . . ."

If Mr. Street suspected too much horseplay from the Scouts at night, he had one means of keeping them out of trouble . . . the Midnight Hike. "Everybody UP!" he would yell, and all the Scouts grabbed their flashlights and off they'd go, Mr. Street leading the way, gone for at least an hour. Keeping in line and walking through spider-webs in the dark sure wore this Scout down, and we were all ready for the comfort of our sleeping bags once we got back to camp.

Not all the tricks were on a grand scale. Some were small and only between a few Scouts, not the whole troop. Duane Tarver recalls the violation of private property on one campout:

"I recall a few times your brother and I may have had some fun at your expense. I remember one time that me and a couple of other guys [I think Ray (Mahaffey) was one of them and maybe Mike Quine.] did some frog gigging late at night at one of the campouts. Well it was late, we did pretty good, and we didn't feel like skinning and cutting the legs off so we stuck a dozen or so of them in your brother's ice chest but didn't bother waking him up for permission. He was very perturbed with me the rest of the weekend waking up to a bunch of bloody frogs when he went to fix breakfast."

14

The Tree Man

Originally written for the Troop 826 website on January 16, 2006

I had just turned 11 at the beginning of the summer of 1968, which meant that now I could officially become a Boy Scout with Troop 826. I could also go on my first camping trip—a weeklong summer camp at Camp Wisdom—and tag along with my big brother David who would get stuck with the task of watching out for me.

I knew many of the troop members already; some were from the old neighborhood on LaSalle Street, others I had gone to school with at A.S. Johnston, and some had come to our house for patrol meetings with David. So I was pretty much in my element except for the fact that I was the youngest member of the troop and everybody else had more experience . . . plus they were bigger than me. Well, that can be a safe place for a little while. Nobody expects anything out of you.

There were also other troops at Camp Wisdom for this week that I wasn't familiar with, including a troop of inner-city Boy Scouts camping across the ravine from us. They were friendly; everybody got along, but I hadn't really been exposed to many city people before, so this was a new experience for me. I guess I led a sheltered life in the suburbs.

I had been following some of the older fellows around all week, listening to what they had to say, watching how they related to others. A few of these older Scouts began telling stories of a "Tree Man," about how a tree had been sighted roaming the different campsites and making raids at night. This was kind of a "Wolf Man" monster, only it was a tree instead that could walk around like a man.

These older Scouts seemed to enjoy telling younger Scouts about the Tree Man. They especially enjoyed telling this story to the Scouts of other troops, including the one inner-city troop. I didn't put much stock in the story, but did notice some who did.

The summer camp went on all week as it should have, up until the last night, when a few of these older Scouts got together for some unknown plans. John Deardorff, one of the kids from the old neighborhood, who I knew to be the fastest runner around, had volunteered to become the Tree Man. Green branches, twigs, and leaves were taken from the nearest trees and tied with twine to John's arms, legs, and torso. When he was covered, he would stand still, looking like a tree, especially at night. He walked away with a few of the older Scouts. What is he going to do?

After a while the excitement began. We heard yelling coming down the path from the older Scouts whose voices I recognized, "The Tree Man!" "He's here!" "He's after me!" "Oh no, he's gonna catch me!" and then the death yell, "Yeaaarrrgghhh!"

I don't know what most of us at 826 were thinking. We were all kind of listening. I guess it was a mass cooperative effort, our silence. But we wanted to hear. We laughed among ourselves.

Then the real screaming began down the trail and across the ravine. We saw flashlights and knew things were moving in the next camp (more laughing among ourselves). This went on for a few minutes, with the noise getting louder. The troop of inner-city Scouts was coming our way, all of them! One thing had not been taken into account—kids from the inner city knew how to fight back.

What am I supposed to do? I'm only 11! I watch; that's all I can do. Nothing's expected of me.

I see this tree figure running through the camp, chased by 50 Boy Scouts with flashlights and knives and axes, all bent on catching the half-man, half-vegetable from hell. John was quick. He could outrun anybody. He ran around the camp with the mob following close on his tail. He ran through the camp. Why didn't he just run out into the woods and blend in? I guess he needed light to see where he was going. He was really doing a good job of running too. He would have gotten away except

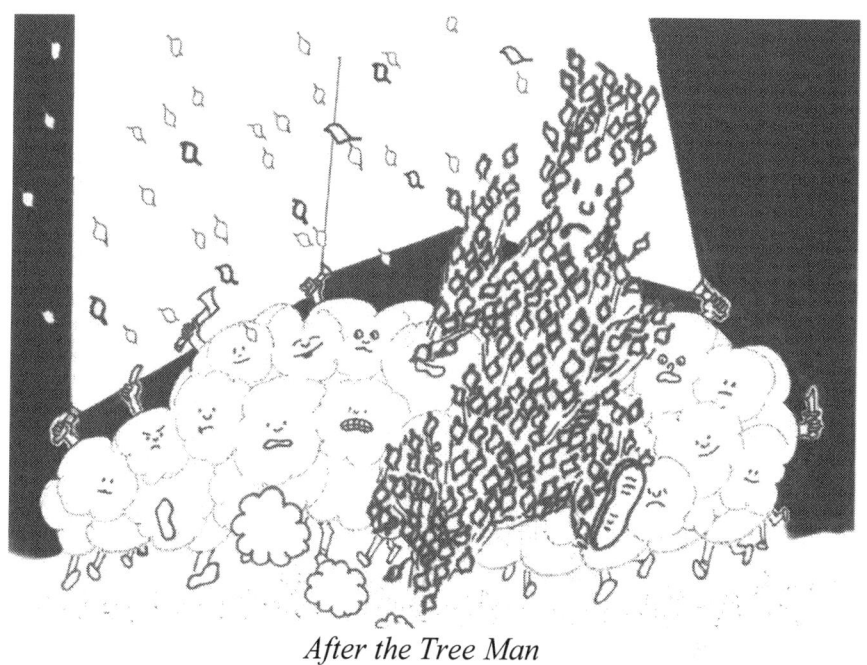

After the Tree Man

for the fact that he ran around a tent where a line had been strung to a peg in the ground. He tripped over that line and "Thud," hit the ground hard, the branches cushioning his fall. All the Scouts from the next-door troop were on him. I thought he was a goner. They brought him up and started pulling leaves, twigs, and branches off of him. They were flying. John was still struggling, but also smirking, trying to get away, trying to hide his face, but of course it was too late. He'd been identified as a man, not a beast. All the flashlights were on him, and he'd been sheared down to his normal self.

Mr. Street jumped in saying, "All right, that's good and well; you caught the Tree Man," before any real harm came to John. I was relieved to see that. But the inner-city Scouts were all laughing too. They'd caught their man and exposed the myth.

I was glad nobody got hurt or killed. Is this what happens at all the Boy Scout camps and Jamborees? Nobody told me about this. These things weren't in the *Boy Scout Handbook*. What happened to the wholesome do-good images presented to us through *Boy's Life Magazine?* I think this way was more fun. There were more raids in the following years, but this was the first I'd experienced.

Being away from home was a time of discovering how other people lived and worked and functioned . . . we came together for a short while in order to cooperate and to learn how to work as a team. Being thrown into the mix and in close contact, we had to get along. This included seeing how others reacted under sudden stress and high anxiety . . . from being scared to death! If nobody got hurt, and I don't recall many instances when anyone was, the laughter somehow had a sudden way of healing any offense. Many were chosen to experience a sudden fear, but it was quickly over. Scouts learned how to laugh at themselves; Scouts had to learn how to forgive—a tough lesson at any age, but better sooner than later. I think many of us remember the pranks more than earning merit badges or rank. Why not? Some of us put more effort into the pranks.

CHAPTER THREE

TROOP HISTORY

A History of Troop 826
Originally written for the Troop 826 website in 2005

THE ONLY PERSON who could give an accurate history of Boy Scout Troop 826 of Irving, Texas, would be its Scoutmaster, Mr. Warren Street. All I can supply here is something from a kid's point of view.

More than 40 years ago, in 1966, my big brother David Bennett joined Troop 826, and for the next 2 years, I had to hear stories about campouts, meetings, merit badges, Courts of Honor, and other tales that made me wish I were older. At that time, the troop was having the weekly meeting in the cafeteria of A.S. Johnston Elementary School on Rutgers Street. I used to see the Scouts there during and after the meetings. I used to watch the meetings at night through the cafeteria window. The Cub Scouts (Pack 669, my pack) had their meetings there, but only on a quarterly basis. I recall David telling me of Gary Nelson, who was the Boy Scout troop leader (the Senior Patrol Leader), and how all the kids looked up to him. I wanted to be a part of this troop. I wanted to belong.

Once during my pre-Scout time, Mr. Street had decided that the responsibilities of being a Scoutmaster had become too great, and he was set to turn it all over to someone else. David told me how all the parents came to one of the meetings and persuaded him not to retire, that the kids all liked and looked up to him. He provided a great outlet for them, plus a service to the community. Organized activities kept many young men in the area from running wild.

"I wanted to be a part of this troop. I wanted to belong."

When I joined Troop 826 in 1968, Mr. Street was still the Scoutmaster. The Scout troop had by then moved to an old church building near Valley View and Walnut Hill Lane, part of the old Estelle Community, next to what would become the present-day DFW Airport. If we were to meet there today, we might be in a flight path and have trouble communicating because of the airplane noise.

In those days, Ray Mahaffey and Jack Rankin were the Scout leaders—the Senior and Assistant Senior Patrol Leaders—and they could run a good meeting. We had a great time, but I didn't really fully appreciate it until years later when I figured out that much of the fun I had in growing up was due to Mr. Street and the Boy Scout troop. I had no idea what goals were or how to attain those goals; others did. But I had fun all the same. That's the main reason I went. Work toward goals? Where was I, at school?

A few times, George Alford, a leader in the Boy Scouts in Irving and a well-known local Native American, came to visit, and we listened and learned something about the American Indian culture.

Mr. Street, Mr. Mahaffey, Mr. Nelson, Mr. Weaver, and Mr. Hart took us places we'd never have seen without the chance to explore. They took the troop swimming at the YMCA in downtown Dallas where the swimming pool was on the second floor (what an engineering feat)! On one weekend trip per month, we went camping on land owned by people affiliated with the Scout troop where we learned (or tried to learn) how to cook and learned about nature and camping, while working toward our next Boy Scout rank. We toured plants and manufacturing sites where we saw industry in action and gained an appreciation for the opportunity in our country.

In the summers, we visited Camp Wisdom, Camp Texoma, Camp Constantin, and, if we were lucky enough, went to the Boy Scout Jamborees (usually for more serious-minded Scouts).

All the leaders who went camping with us had their own gear and equipment, which was far superior to anything we had. They could drive of course, so they'd have their pickup trucks packed with gear, and the leaders would keep to their own little part of the campsite. That was where the best cooking occurred. Mr. Street loved cooking, and he made use of a Dutch oven. (Who had the patience to cook? As a kid, I would just put a hotdog on a wire and call that lunch—no clean up, no mess!) But the adult leadership would have apple cobbler and roast beef, and they'd have a whole pantry off the back of Mr. Street's truck with salt, pepper, spices, catsup, and other things that we boys didn't think to bring.

I left the Boy Scouts in the early 1970s and came back to visit for a short while after that when Chuck Wagner and Jerry Thetford were running the troop. I was amazed at how smoothly they ran the meetings still being held at the old church. But at that time, I still wasn't focused and had no idea what leadership or goals were all about, so I got involved in other things: like surviving public school, mainly.

A few years ago, I apologized to Mr. Street for not sticking with the program, for not going all the way to Eagle Scout. He said, "Well, it's not like Scouting was an Eagle Factory." He's right. If you were among the more serious-minded, goal-oriented Scouts, you could make it to Order of the Arrow and on up to Eagle. I congratulate them! They deserved it. Mr. Street stayed with Troop 826 until sometime in the mid-to-late 1970s when he decided it was time to give it up. There were Scouts before and after my involvement; I wish I could have known them all but that was impossible. About a year or so ago, I saw a lady with her sons in a local store. She was dressed in some kind of Scout-colored blouse. I looked closer at the patch on her shoulder, which read "826." I talked to her, saying how I was affiliated with 826 some 30+ years before (maybe around the time she was born!). She asked me who the Scoutmaster was at that time, and I said Warren Street. She said she knew who he was and that he had cooked for them (all the Scoutmasters, I presume) at Camp Wisdom at a meeting. So

Mr. Street is still cooking, still involved in Scouting, even in this new millennium.

This short history is all from a kid's point of view. Someone else can fill in the year, places, and details.

The Scout Hut

When the Scouts began meeting as Troop 826, they gathered at the cafeteria of the elementary school A.S. Johnston, located at 2801 Rutgers Drive. They did this for a few years until around 1967 when a more suitable place was found for young men in Scouting outside of the settled area of Irving, entering the country, in the old community of Estelle. It wasn't long after that Estelle was incorporated into the Irving city limits.

Whenever I want to know something about Irving, especially people or the old area of Irving I'm not familiar with, I get in touch with the Irving Public Library. I've driven there many times, but I find that communicating by e-mail saves me wear and tear. The library has an Archives section directed by Jan Hart. She and Kevin Kendro manage to have answers for whatever questions I send their way.

I asked them about the old churches or schools in the Estelle community, and they told me that a two-story framed Masonic lodge and school building was built there in 1884. I knew that the Scout Hut we used was a one-story building; this couldn't be it. They then wrote that a brick school building had been erected in 1916 and even sent me a photograph. Again, this couldn't be the one because the building we had used for Scout meetings was made of wood. Then they told me, "In 1942, they [the Estelle Community] built a new one-story frame school building almost due west of the brick building." This made sense to me, because I had seen two foundations for two buildings, one larger foundation for a brick building (to the east), and concrete for piers where the 1942 building stood. These piers were where we Scouts met at the Scout Hut during the late 1960s and into the 1970s. So the Scout Hut had originally been built as a school and used as a church in later years.

The Scout Hut was a one-story building, located just outside of the (then) Irving city limits, just off of Valley View Lane and within sight of Walnut Hill Lane. It was located in the country, and within a couple of years, DFW Airport would open just across the street from Valley View. The land for the airport had already been purchased and was in the process of being fenced off during our Scouting years.

The Hut was made entirely of wood, and it was on a pier and beam foundation. The rectangular building ran from east and west, parallel to Estelle Road just north of it, and the two entrances were in the middle of the building on the north and south side; windows were on the south side only. The north entrance had a concrete one-step porch, while the back entrance had a much bigger four- or five-step concrete porch, since there was a slope away from the road towards the Harrington Cemetery, which was about 50 yards south of the Scout Hut. We rarely ventured into the cemetery. We were happy to just play in the big field in the back (south side) of the Hut. There were mesquite trees in the area. The yards surrounding the Scout Hut were mowed, but if you went more than 100 feet away from it, the grass was over knee high.

Inside the school/Scout Hut/church the floors were made of hardwood. They took a beating when we were there, since many times we were forced to play indoors due to wet or cold conditions during winter. There was a chalkboard on the east wall. There were wooden pews, perhaps a dozen, which faced the chalkboard. The pews weren't the heavy solid-oak brand

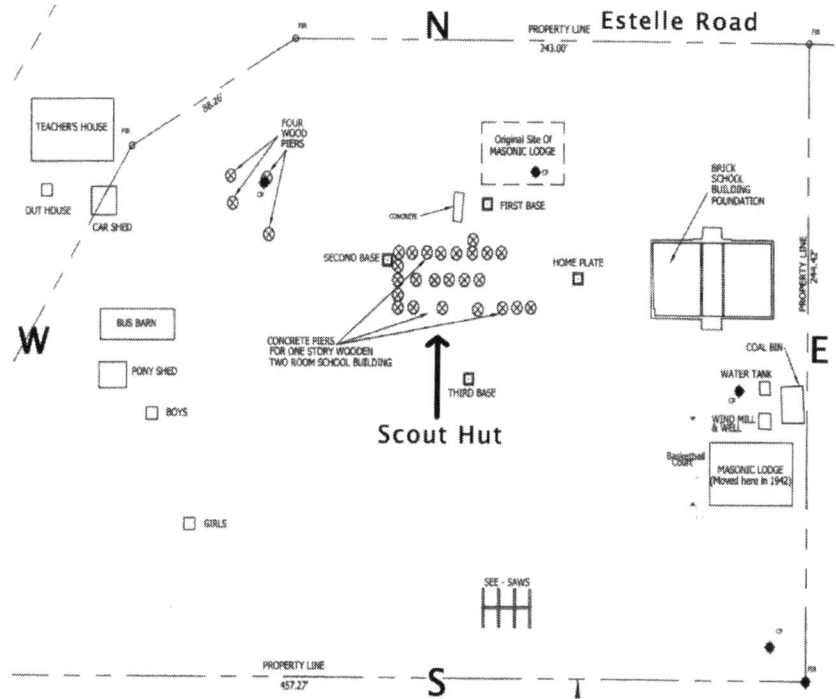

Scout Hut Map. A portion of the Estelle Community, now incorporated into Irving, Texas. Provided by Jan Hart and Kevin Kendro, Irving Public Library Archivists.

you'd find in your established churches. These pews were 15-feet long and made of slats with spaces between them. They were much lighter weight and could be moved by Scouts, one on each end. There was no middle aisle. The pews were in the middle, and there was about 4 feet on either side of the pews between the end of the pew and the walls—space enough for people to walk. There was an open space for the teacher or preacher by the chalkboard, maybe 12 feet, enough room to move around in. Two pews were on the north and south side in this area, backs to the wall, facing the preacher/pulpit area. I suppose this is where the deacons, elders, or choir sat.

The pews took up only half of the building, the east side. There was an open area on the west side, with a small stage at the end, but I don't remember it ever being used by the Scouts. Whenever we had a picnic or a Court of Honor, the food was served on that side of the building. We kids would gather our food from this area quickly and take it outside to eat, where we could spill our drinks and spit watermelon seeds with abandon; nobody had to clean it up out there.

The Scout Hut had no indoor restroom, and I don't recall seeing an outdoor restroom, either. There was an old-looking shack of a building standing at the west side of the Scout Hut, but I always assumed that was a tool shed. Whenever one of us had business to attend to, he'd take a long walk in the high grass area and find a mesquite tree.

It was a great place to be a Scout—close enough to civilization, but just outside of the city so we could be a part of nature. Even if we didn't own it, it was like having a place of our own. It wasn't ours as a troop, but we had an appreciation for it.

Where the Scout Hut stood. I'm in the picture
for human scale (6'1").

Recently I've driven out to where the Scout Hut used to be, just off Valley View Lane, which divides the old Estelle Community from the DFW Airport. I could hear the bulldozers; they are getting closer to the area. I don't know how much longer the Estelle Preservation Society will be able to hold on to this property. It's doubtful that the Harrington Cemetery will be built over, but it may be the only plot, fenced in, to survive. Most of Irving is concrete now, with highways covering its once-open pasture and grazing land. The concrete supports for the piers of the Scout Hut are still visible, but that's all.

Mark Dixon, one of the Scouts from the earliest years of Troop 826, recalls the games and activities we played inside and outside around the Scout Hut. He recalls one story in particular:

"I remember a lot of neat things we did. We got out there and played games—Crab Hockey, Steal the Bacon—and I remember one of the games was Foxes and Hounds, and one of the memories that get indelibly etched in your brain, and as I describe this you'll understand why. Someone had dug a giant pit out there, about 50 yards behind the Scout Hut. I don't know if it was part of a drainage ditch or whatever, but it was fairly deep, and it had water in it. I remember it was in the wintertime, and we were out there playing, and several of us were running down through there to hide. It was me and several others; I can't remember who all went in with me. We were running down through the field, and the next thing we knew, we were flying through the air, and then we're underwater. That water was freezing cold, and all I remember was sheer panic . . . and trying to claw my way out of there. The water wasn't all that deep, but when you're suddenly in cold water, and you don't know where the bottom is, and you're clawing for the edges, and we came out of that thing all drenched. It seemed that there were two or three of us. It was one of those memories that, wow."

In the general area that Mark describes, the Harrington Cemetery still exists, just south of the Scout Hut property line. There were no fences at that time; it was just a large field with the cemetery across the property line. Mark may have run and fallen into an open and, at that time, unused grave, which had filled with water from the rain. I'm not saying that he did, but the possibility for this happening is strong.

I asked Mark how Mr. Street reacted when he reported back to the Scout Hut after recreation, what his reaction had been to Mark being dripping wet. Mark said, "He was always, he was great. I don't remember. Very seldom did we have reprimands. If anything, he would turn things into teaching moments."

Teaching moments. It was almost an honor to be corrected by Mr. Street. We Scouts had a healthy respect for authority as long as we respected the source. There was a lot of correcting done at the old Scout Hut.

Winter Campout 1969. Rodney Street, Mark Dixon,
Mark Null, Mike Reed, Lincoln Monroe

CHAPTER FOUR

SCOUTMASTER WARREN STREET

WARREN STREET WAS KNOWN as a good Scoutmaster because he understands the concepts of justice and dignity and independence, which are not common traits or on display much in these times. Mr. Street is a good man. I had a chance to question him about his life and the troop, but I found that he'd rather talk about the troop than himself. The Scouts I spoke to agree that Mr. Street was the leader we needed to keep the troop running and the kids in line.

Mr. Street's involvement with the troop was inspiring, and for those of us who had the privilege to learn from him, we know his contribution and guidance cannot be measured. In his own words,

"My Scouting started when my son Richard joined the Boy Scouts in 1964. I became active in Scouting too by becoming the Assistant Scoutmaster in Troop 826. John Alexander was the Scoutmaster at that time. A year after that, James Butterworth became the new Scoutmaster. Approximately a year later, I became the Scoutmaster of the troop. I kept records of all our activities from that time, which would become important later in years. We regularly had a campout each month come rain or shine. Each year we attended a weeklong summer camp at several Scout camps served by the council. One of the favorite camps was located on Possum Kingdom Lake. On each campout, the boys would work on various merit badges that were required in advancement towards the Eagle rank. Rodney, my number-two son, also became a Scout and advanced to the rank of Star. The troop earned money that was used in buying needed equipment by collecting newspapers, collecting scrap metal, [and] picking up trash along the city streets for $1 a bag. We were able to buy all the tentage, cookware, and camp trailer. We camped at several farms and ranches during the 13 or more years. Favorite spots were the Dixon farm in Melissa, Texas; the Johnson ranch in Meridian, Texas; Sid Richardson Scout Reservation at Lake Bridgeport; Lake Texoma; a farm in Terrell, Texas; Clements Scout Reservation in Athens, Texas; and many other sites that include Oklahoma, Leonard, and Worth Ranch in the Longhorn Council. The troop record books indicate campouts and other activities such as conservation projects, Scout shows and parades. Other camps included Borah Farm, Lake Murray, Pipes Farm, Lewis Farm, Ford Ranch, Bennett Land, [and] Grapevine Lake. Ray Mahaffey organized a trip to NASA and Ellington Air Force Base in Houston for his Eagle project. When Troop 826 deactivated, the monies left over were spent on bowling at Triangle Bowl in Irving, pizza suppers at Shotgun Sam's, and spaghetti suppers at Spaghetti Warehouse in Dallas' West End.

Mr. Warren Street, Scoutmaster (l.) and
Mr. Bob Nelson, Assistant Scoutmaster (r.), July 1966

On my 80th birthday, February 22, 2003, I was surprised by a big birthday party at the house, having many of the former Scouts from Troop 826 show up at the door. On my 83rd birthday former Scouts of the troop surprised me again with a birthday party. Eight former Scouts plus two of the fathers came. Mike Quine created a website for Troop 826 and that was another surprise. It gives much of the history of the troop with campout topics, campfire tales, and other topics of interest. It's a great tribute to me and to the troop."

Mr. Street was born at home in Rochester, New York, on Washington's Birthday, 1923, to Fred and Minnie Street. I asked Mr. Street about his early years, what his father did for a living, about his family, and was surprised to find that he was somewhere in the middle of nine children, a few of whom are still with us. Mr. Street remarked that his father was a "jack of all trades, master of none," like many of us. He did what he could, found work where it existed, and his mother stayed at home to care for the children. She would cook over the wood stove where Mr. Street learned some of his cooking skills, and if you weren't at the table when the meal was served, then you went hungry. The children learned how to be prompt that way! Minnie Street would tell Warren to go out and get a chicken, kill it, and prepare it for supper . . . so Mr. Street learned the skills of survival starting from the care of animals all the way to the dinner table. He would later share this knowledge to us suburban Scouts by taking a live chicken on campouts. That weekend we learned our meals didn't originate from cellophane-wrapped packages at the local grocery store. He also shot wild rabbits in the nearby woods as a youngster for food. In a family of nine children, you learned how to be productive. These were the days before government assistance was handed out like candy—the family was the unit of survival.

Mike Huebner, a Scout who came along during the middle of 826's existence, tells of learning where poultry meat came from:

"You know some of that is foggy to me . . . the way I remember it, I'm not sure it's the way it happened; one of the favorite things of all time I remember is, we were on a campout . . . and really that's what I loved about the Scouts, was the campouts. But it was in the morning, and Mr. Street, he had a teepee, or maybe it was a tent, and when he came out of this teepee, he was all dressed up in Indian clothes, you know, the headband,

Troop 826 Reunion Party, February 22, 2006.
Front row: Mike Huebner, Hilton Quine, Richard Bennett.
Second row: Alvin Brown, Jerry Thetford, Mr. Street,
Monte Pipes, Mr. Mahaffey. Back row: Mark Dixon,
Steve Rackley, Richard Salas, Jack Rankin.

the whole bit. He came out with a live chicken and a tomahawk! Do you remember that? Well I remember; he comes out with the chicken and ax and there was a stump there, a tree stump, he puts this chicken on top there, and he gives this bloodcurdling scream and chopped his head off, and the chicken went running around with its head chopped off, and we were just rolling around laughing . . . remember that? I remember dodging it! It ran around, that memory has been ingrained in me . . .! Oh, yeah, I loved Mr. Street; I thought he was great!"

I asked Mr. Street about dressing up as a Native American when killing a chicken, but he said he only dressed up for Scout ceremonial purposes, not for food preparation.

Mr. Street joined the Army Air Corp at the beginning of WWII in 1942 and stayed with the Air Force for 20 years until he retired in the early 1960s. He married Mary Lura McGee in 1951, saw military service in Germany, Japan, Korea, and Panama, and had two sons, Richard and Rodney.

After leaving the Air Force, he worked at Continental Trailways for a year, then hired on to the Xerox Corporation, staying with them for 24 and a half years, retiring again in the late 1980s.

During his second career was when he decided to become involved as a supporter, then later a Scoutmaster, to Troop 826, beginning with his son Richard's induction into the Boy Scouts.

I asked Mr. Street about his physical appearance once; we Scouts found that he was the epitome of 'physically strong, mentally awake, and morally straight.' I think he had retained a sense of military demeanor from his days in the Air Force. He wasn't aloof; we didn't salute him or act too formal around him . . . it was just that he carried himself differently from other men his age. He didn't let himself get slovenly, overweight, or sloppy in appearance. He was in better shape at age 50 than many of us Scouts in our teens! He answered me by saying he started weightlifting while in Japan; he didn't want to be picked on or to look like an easy target, and he just kept exercising since then. He was shoulders, had a "V" physique, kind of like the actor Robert Conrad, only with less hair. His appearance may be why the Scouts would listen to him when he spoke; they wanted to be like him when they became an adult. He came with a few military tattoos on his arms, but he didn't favor them. I heard him remark once how he wished he'd never gotten them. Because of his health-consciousness, he was able to keep up with and in many cases surpass the energy of the Scouts.

Concerning respect and admiration for Mr. Street, I asked Chuck Wagner how he managed to become Senior Patrol Leader; Chuck remarked:

"You know, I don't really know; it just seemed like the natural progression. Mr. Street was always very supportive of me and any of the other kids. The thing that I recall most in that regard was that Mr. Street would always make sure that if you had a job to do, you had to do the job. If you volunteered to do something, or if you wanted to do something, it was expected that you would meet the obligations of it. And of course as we've talked about before, Mr. Street had that effect on boys— they really wanted to live up to his expectations of them. That's what I found myself doing, when I got into being the Assistant Patrol Leader. By gosh, I was going to be the best Assistant Patrol Leader I could be, and the same thing on up the line. So I think by the time the Senior Patrol Leader spot was available or needed to be filled, I think I'd probably done, in Mr. Street's eyes, a decent job of any position beforehand that he thought I could handle the SPL."

Staff Sergeant Warren Street (USAF), circa 1955

Once on a campout, Chuck was trying to earn his Camping merit badge, and one of the requirements was that he was supposed to prepare a shelter for himself to sleep in, away from the rest of the troop, out in the wild. When Mr. Street came around to rate the shelters, he saw that Chuck's wasn't as strong as it should be and tested it as a storm would by helping it to collapse. Chuck had to rebuild his shelter, but he did it better the second time. Chuck says,

"I didn't know what I was learning at the time. I couldn't put it into words at the time, but that's when I learned that being brave is not the absence of fear. It's feeling the fear and doing it anyway, because you have to, you need to, or you want to. I would not have learned that lesson if Mr. Street had not come along and told me what a cruddy, awful shelter I had built and knocked it to the ground. If he had come up and said, "Oh well, that's not bad; you did a real fine job trying there, Mr. Wagner," I wouldn't have been out there that night! I wouldn't have had enough respect for him that it would have mattered to me what he thought about whether or not I went out there that night.

I was mad as all get-out, but I wasn't mad at him! He knocked it down and said it was a horrible shelter. I knew that! I was just mad at myself because I knew that I hadn't done a very good job, and I wasn't mad at Mr. Street for knocking it down. I was mad at me for not doing a better job! Well, *that's* what a leader does; that's what a man can teach a boy—that kind of self-analysis and self-respect. Mr. Street was brave enough himself, that when he would catch you doing something wrong, he wouldn't sugarcoat it. He would tell you, "That ain't good enough!" "That's wrong!" "You didn't do it right!" So many times so many people will try to sugarcoat things for kids, not ruffle feathers. Mr. Street would whack you right between the eyes with a 2 x 4 and say, "Get in there and do it again!""

When I asked him about what he took with him from his Scouting experiences, Chuck went on to tell me about what he'd learned from Mr. Street:

"You've mentioned Mr. Street and our friendship there, and obvious that's something I treasure more than anything. I feel our relationship has been very similar to father and son, he was like a second dad to me, and the things that I think I took away with my time with Mr. Street, one of the things—anyone who knows him will tell you is—he has opinions . . . he'll usually let you know what they are. One of the things I took away from that was the appreciation to know your own mind, and to have principles, to stand up for them, whether you're popular or not popular from them. I may have learned tact from a few other Scout Leaders along the way . . . but from Mr. Street I definitely learned to know what you believe in, stand up for it, fight for it.

I think as a boy, as a young guy, it's so vital that we have grown men we can look to that are strong, that have principles, that have beliefs, and who don't apologize for who they are, who will tell you straight up this is the way it is, and they're not afraid to tell you if you come up short, you come up short! I think that's one of the things I appreciate most from Mr. Street was he set the bar very high, and he expected you to get there. The expectations from him were never low, they were always high, they were always attainable. And the thing is, most kids who were 10, 11, 12, 13 years old don't even know what they're capable of, and Mr. Street did, so he'd set the bar high, and invariably, because kids are kids, they'd fail. They'd fail sometimes, they'd succeed sometimes, and the way they succeed from the failure. He would not let up, he would make sure you gave it everything you had, and that's what I learned, the meaning of success from him—to give it everything you have, do the best you can, and if something doesn't work out the way it should, go back and try again. Do something a little different. Don't give up. If you've got an objective, if you've got a goal, you need to be there and do it!"

Jerry Thetford, a Scout in Troop 826 during its last years, recalls his then-and-now impressions of Mr. Street:

"My dad was pretty strict with us; he made sure we did the right thing, that we took responsibility for our actions. Mr. Street reinforced that; that was the way he was. He was like my second father. He's as close as my father is to me. He was strict, but he still let you have fun, as long as you weren't hurting anybody or getting into too much serious trouble. He was all for having fun or wrestling around with the boys, that sort of thing, but if you got out of line, he'd put you back in your place! I see a lot of kids nowadays who don't get the discipline that we had while we were growing up; it's a different time now . . . and Mr. Street was a little older than my father maybe by about 10 years, so he was a different generation from my father, so he grew up during the Depression; he saw the hard times, and uh, he wasn't just a woman!

Mr. Street taught us so much. He made us earn our way. We weren't sponsored by anyone. We weren't sponsored by a church, a school, or anyone. We were our own sponsors: the only way we made money was if we earned it! Between collecting newspapers, scrapping metal, and picking up trash along the side of the road, we had to earn all the money we needed. I was talking to my dad about this the other night—how Mr. Street, you know I got to thinking of what was so important to the Scouts, to me, you know, was it the program, or the camping, or exactly what it was, and then it finally came to me that the reason Scouting was so important to me and that

I got so much out of it was because of one person, and that one person was Mr. Street. It was just the way he led the troop and the way he loved the boys. You could tell he did. Even after his boys got out of Scouting he continued to do it, and he made such a difference to me in my life. It was because of him that I enjoyed Scouting. I'll never forget him as long as I live, that's for sure. He's a great man. I love him to death. I always will. You know as well as I do, he was important to your life I'm sure, or you wouldn't be doing this story about Troop 826, because really, Mr. Street was Troop 826. [Scouting] definitely helped me take responsibility for the things I do."

Jerry's Scouting experiences were so favorable that he gave a few years back as a Scoutmaster in the city he later settled in, Azle. I found this kind of interesting because Jerry was by then a working man, married, with three daughters and no sons. Many Scoutmasters get involved because they have sons in the troop, but here's a man who, out of gratitude, wanted to give back to the kids what Mr. Street and the volunteers gave him. Jerry recalls:

"It wasn't until after I got out of the Air Force and moved back to Texas, along about 1992 or 93, I got back into the Boy Scouts, and I was an Assistant Scoutmaster for a while, then I was the Scoutmaster for about 3 years with a local troop here, Troop 334, and I just loved the program so much when in it as a boy that I wanted to try to give some of it back to the younger boys that were coming up now . . . I always felt inadequate, though, as a leader, as a Scoutmaster, because I . . ."

When I suggested that we couldn't all be like Mr. Street, Jerry said,

"That's what it was! I kept looking back at Mr. Street and how he did things, and I'll never be as good as he is, I'll never be the kind of man he was to Troop 826. He obviously loved it."

In speaking with my brother David Bennett, he revealed that at one time he thought all families were intact, with one Dad, one Mom, happy kids, just like on television in those days. He soon discovered that many boys didn't have what we had at home, which was a form of stability. Mr. Street had a way of becoming a role model, as David recalls:

"[Mr. Street] was a second dad to a lot of us! I mean he was out there taking care of us and making sure that we were, uh, just making sure we were behaving. By gosh, he was policing us all the time, watching out for us. It's not like he was a Nazi commandant strutting around and stuff. He loved to have a good laugh, but he sure wasn't afraid of putting his boot in your butt if you needed it. He was always looking out for our safety. I don't think I realized it at the time, but he was always looking out for us. Being that I'm 50+ years old now I understand that, but at the time I thought he was just snooping on us, actually bothering us in a way. He felt a tremendous responsibility to our parents, I'm sure, to make sure we got back intact, not too much worse for the wear. He was a strong male influence, a strong male role model that I know some of the guys didn't have. Mr. Street was a person who had strong beliefs who wasn't afraid to share what his beliefs were, and if you were doing substandard work, you'd know about it because he'd tell you about it! He didn't suffer fools. I recall once when Mr. Street was talking about stepping down as Scoutmaster (in the mid-60s). I hated to see that because, you know, I love the man. He was a big part of the troop, and I was the first one to realize that he told us, after he'd met with the parents that night at A.S.

Johnston where they'd promised him more parental support; he pulled all the boys together and said, "Well boys, you're looking at your new Scoutmaster." I was the first one to cheer "All right!" because I knew exactly what he was talking about!"

I asked Mike Huebner if he had any suggestions or criticisms of the current Boy Scout programs, any recommendations he could make that would help the Scouts. Mike had only one recommendation when I spoke with him, and it was quite simple, "I would suggest keeping it like it was when Mr. Street was the Scoutmaster." I think that speaks volumes about what we all felt for that man, as Mike said, if there was one influential person in the Scouting program that really affected him, it was "Mr. Street. I've always admired him."

Mr. Street remained Scoutmaster until the late 1970s, when he decided he couldn't run the troop anymore. I asked him his reasons for relinquishing control, and he said that he needed parental support, but that it just wasn't there. One man can't run a troop by himself. This was a sad commentary on our times: the breakup of the family also led to the disintegration of the troop. There was a time we'd have two or three fathers go with us on campouts, giving their support, and being a part of the authority figures. I asked Mr. Street if he'd still be a Scoutmaster today if he could. He said maybe, because sometimes he missed it; he missed all the fun.

I spoke with Mark Dixon, asking him about the people who supported him in the Scouting program and if he thought scouting was a help to him; Mark replied:

"I think we were. All of us helped each other in one manner or another. Certainly Mr. Street was an awesome person to us all.

Mr. Quine and Mr. Mahaffey, I remember they were a large part of our enjoyment and encouraging us to continue getting merit badges and what have you. I know it had to have been a lot out of their time, because having gone through this thing called "life," and having to make a living, [and] raise kids, I know it wasn't easy for me . . . and they really went above and beyond to do all of those things for all of us guys. They didn't have to do it. It was awesome."

Mark told one story about Mr. Street, showing both Mr. Street's sense of humor and good health. He said that on one campout he was outside early in the morning, and Mr. Street was cooking breakfast by the fire. Mark did something, but he didn't quite remember what it was, but he knew he had done something bad enough to make Mr. Street mad. He could tell that by the way Mr. Street suddenly turned and looked at him. (He might have remarked about Mr. Street's male-pattern baldness, something always sure to set him off . . . something both Mark and I suffer today). Anyhow, Mark took off running away from the breakfast fire with Mr. Street in hot pursuit. Mark was sure he could lose him, but Mr. Street wasn't about to give up that easily. Also, Mr. Street was carrying a handful of uncooked bread dough, so Mark knew he had to make his escape. Unfortunately for Mark, the clearing ran out and the forest began, and he was slowed by the trees and brush. By the time Mr. Street caught up to him, Mark was laughing so hard he could not make his escape. Mr. Street wound up smearing the bread dough in Mark's laughing face, which I'm sure helped him remember to respect his elders in the coming years. This was a story I enjoyed, since in years past, I remembered seeing other Scouts trying to outrun Mr. Street. Some of them were successful, others were not. The ones who escaped were usually given a 'pass,' since Mr. Street could easily have caught them. I guess he didn't want to waste any energy on the chase and felt it was just worth it to see the Scout in error running for cover.

I talked with Mark about his remembrances of our campouts and what he took with him from his Scouting experiences. This is a bit of what he shared with me:

"I remember times when we, I think Mr. Street started this as well, he would take biscuit dough and stamp a hole in it and throw it in a pan of grease, and once it came out of there all nice and brown, he'd toss it in a paper sack with powdered sugar, and we'd have our own doughnuts . . . there just wasn't anything better.. . . He taught all of us how to make cobblers and things like that with the Dutch oven. I can't tell you how many people over the years I would show how to cook with a Dutch oven. And teaching my own kids to cook over a fire, the fish fries we've had down at Grapevine Lake on campouts, get down to the lake and catch perch and bring them back up and scale them and put them in skillets, it was just awesome. The hikes that a bunch of us would go on, going out to Possum Kingdom Lake, and chasing girls, because the campsites were close to each other out there. It was either Possum Kingdom or Lake Arrowhead, I can't remember which one it was. We had so many good memories—swimming, and all the different things . . . Canoeing merit badge, all the guys getting together and having a blast. . . . I hardly remember anything that was not a good memory—the times that we would make Mr. Street mad. Somehow or another he always had some way of turning the worst into the best; even if he was reprimanding us, he would somehow do it in a way that we were all were proud to be there. We were proud to be a part."

Mr. Street related that George Alford, an older local man, a Native American, had been an inspiration to him as far as the Boy Scouts were concerned. Mr. Alford was always available to help the Boy Scouts, so I'm assuming that's what Mr. Street admired about him. When he was Scoutmaster, Mr. Street was still holding a full-time job, his second career at the Xerox Corporation in the area, but he still had time to be at the weekly meetings, get his training with the Circle Ten Council, meet with the other adults concerning finances and plans, and make it to our monthly campouts, plus summer camps. He did have an 8-to-5 job, Monday through Friday, which made scheduling a little easier, but still, he didn't have to do all of this.

He tried to keep the Scouts on the straight and narrow, especially when we were on campouts and prone to get into arguments and fights with each other. I don't recall seeing anyone getting into any fights in front of Mr. Street; it may have been that any trouble was averted by his presence. Maybe we knew what would happen to us if we fought over something petty, which is why we would fight among ourselves whenever he wasn't around.

Chapel was a part of our Sunday morning routine in camp, since being away from home we'd miss going to church. We'd have breakfast, clean up, and then Mr. Street and some of the Dad volunteers would march us out away from our campsite to a place under a tree where we'd be more comfortable. A Scout swore an allegiance to God and country, so Mr. Street would make sure we kept our word. He wasn't a minister, and I think he felt himself inadequate to give a sermon or a lecture, so we would participate in a reading, a liturgical-type service. This was my first experience seeing this; I was more used to someone giving a devotional, but I didn't mind. It was interesting. There were no sermons on our part, but the mission had been accomplished. Mr. Street wasn't going to allow his

Scouts' minds to wander. He felt holding Chapel was a Scoutmaster's responsibility to his troop, and he did not shrink from it.

Mr. Street, a District Award of Merit recipient, stayed active with the local Boy Scout program. His skills as a cook are well known, and he has served in that capacity for others on campouts including the adults on the Troop 826 reunion campout. In the past few years, he served along with other volunteers in the construction of the Jim Ince Outdoor Amphitheater, a 700-seat brick, stone, and concrete meeting place for a variety of camp programs . . . also wheelchair accessible. He is named on their plaque of appreciation at the entry point of the Amphitheatre, along with Jim Ince, and several other volunteers.

A few weeks ago, I drove by to see Mr. Street for a few minutes. There he was out in his front yard with his weed whacker tending to his yard at age 86. His exercise and dedication to good health had paid off, and he was still independent, working like a much younger man, enjoying the benefits of fitness. I only hope I can be that way when I hit his age bracket. He's still setting the example.

I'm sure I could call Mr. Street 'Warren' these days, since I'm well into my 50s, and I think he'd let me. He might even recognize me as an adult. However, it wouldn't feel right, and I think I'll just keep on calling him Mr. Street. It's a sign of respect. He deserves it. It would almost be like calling my father by his first name, something I would never do.

CHAPTER FIVE

THE BOY SCOUT OATH AND LAW

The Boy Scout Oath

On my honor I will do my best
To do my duty to God and my country
and to obey the Scout Law;
To help other people at all times;
To keep myself physically strong,
mentally awake, and morally straight.

A View of the Boy Scout Oath

The powerful oath of the Boy Scouts is probably one of the most clear and memorable promises of any organization. Compared with the Pledge of Allegiance, the Serviceman's Oath, and ever-changing wedding vows, this short piece has held up over the years as a request for high standards. It has served as an entry gate to the Scouting program for generations of Boy Scouts. Here is a piece-by-piece view of this promise:

On my honor: Did I know what honor was when I said this as a Scout? I took it to mean I would do my best. I wasn't aware that I had any characteristics near the word "honor." This ties in closely with the next phrase.

I will do my best: Actually, I was just becoming aware of what "best" was—that there was "good," "better," and "best" in myself. Best usually cost something, so I had learned to be comfortable with good enough. I suppose I could have aimed higher.

To do my duty: This meant I had a responsibility. Responsibility was a concept I hadn't yet mastered. It was a slippery concept; and at times, it still is.

To God and my country: These two seemed very close at times, two ideas that were much bigger than anything I'd experienced. God the Sovereign and Country the People. This line makes it plain that I owed something to both.

And to obey the Scout Law: There are twelve characteristics that help define the Scout—good traits to be known by which define how boys should be if they wanted to become useful and productive men, something that would honor both God and country.

To help other people at all times: What a big demand. This may be impossible for one Scout to do all the time, but when working with other Scouts it falls within the realm of possibility. The Boy Scouts are known as a service organization because they strive to help others.

To keep myself physically strong: This is a good practice at any age. As we progress, we have to learn and relearn how to keep ourselves active and healthy. This Scout has never been an athlete, but has been reasonably healthy, so this portion of the oath was viewed as reasonable. Why the health requirement? So we can help other people at all times! If we let ourselves and our health go, others will be required to help us, and that's not productive.

Mentally awake: To stay up with current events, to learn to understand, and to seek education where and when we are able. Not all of us are in academics, but there's no end to learning no matter in what area we find ourselves.

And morally straight: This is a lifetime struggle, not just something for the Scouting years. Learning the difference between right and wrong, choosing the path that's right, and keeping ourselves at a peak enables us to help others. Dealing fairly with others is something that's taught early among the Cub Scouts. I hope I don't sound like I'm preaching at you. It's just that this promise requires a great deal from a Scout, and perhaps he should know that.

The Scout Law

A Scout is:

Trustworthy
Loyal
Helpful
Friendly
Courteous
Kind
Obedient
Cheerful
Thrifty
Brave
Clean
Reverent

A View of the Scout Law

There are twelve parts to this one Scout Law. Maybe this should be referred to as the Scout Laws. These characteristics are not natural. No one is born with the following traits; they must be learned. These are good choices for Scouts to strive for in order to grow up to be a benefit to others:

Trustworthy: Can a Scout be trusted? Is he worthy of trust? Trust is something to be earned; it is closely tied to honor and honesty. The Scout has to learn this or perhaps pick it up from the example of others. (Hopefully from good leadership!)

Loyal: How does a Scout learn loyalty? Probably the same way he learns to be trustworthy. A quick lesson in loyalty can be gained by observing the family pet, Fido (for 'faithful').

Helpful: The Scout wants to be a help, an aid to those less able or fortunate, beginning in the home, then the community.

Friendly: Young men must work on appearing and being friendly. If you look at a boy in a Scout uniform, there's no worry about him getting into trouble. He makes friends by being a friend.

Courteous: The same goes for courtesy. He extends courtesy and respect to others, even before it's earned, giving others the opportunity to reciprocate.

Kind: Kindness to all members of the family, the troop, community—and this should extend even to the humane treatment of animals.

Obedient: The Scout learns to obey those who have charge over him, whether at home, school, on the job, or in the troop. At this stage in life, he should be learning, and he cannot do that if he is causing disruptions through disobedience.

Cheerful: If all the laws are observed, then the Scout should have good reason to be cheerful. He is finding his niche in life. The fewer problems he has to deal with, the more cheerful he can be toward others. He will be as a shining light; other Scouts will want to be like him.

Thrifty: The Scout needs to realize that his resources are limited, and he should learn how to handle his finances in a way that is not wasteful. In learning to handle his finances now, he may be able to support himself and others in his family one day and not be a burden on others.

Summer Camp at Sid Richardson Scout Ranch, 1970.

Brave: A Scout learns to recognize his own fear, but he carries out his duties and responsibilities anyway.

Clean: Cleanliness is next to godliness; is it an accident that this law is listed next to reverence? A Scout works on keeping himself clean, physically as well as mentally and morally.

Reverent: The Scout recognizes his need for God, and strives toward obedience and reverence.

Troop 826 on the Oath and Law

Jerry Thetford said, "I'm a big believer in the Boy Scout program, the values that it instills, the Scout Law and the Scout Oath. These are important things to know and do. If you can live the Scout Oath and the Scout Law, I truly believe you'll be a better individual, a better citizen."

I asked Mark Dixon whether he thought Scouting had a positive negative impact on his life, and he summed it up like this:

"I think, to a great extent, everything along the way in your life supports values that you learned, and friendships, and lessons which you've learned; all of those things were a whole lot less likely to be imprinted without the incidents of Scouting being in our lives. Just like the Prodigal Son, as kids get older they kind of veer away from what they've learned and have been taught. Eventually, hopefully they come back to those values and basics that have been taught to them when they were younger. Scouting is one of those things that had a great impact on all of us to give us values, to help us know what was normal. So many of us had very dysfunctional lives and home lives, and lack of people skills and what have you, and I think

Scouting filled a very necessary part of our lives in the process."

Later in our conversation, Mark and I discussed the Oath and the Law and what they mean to Scouts. Mark said:

"I think some of the things in the Scout Oath and Scout Motto may have changed a little bit from what they were from when we were Scouts. I really liked the way the Scout Oath and the list of items that are indicative of a Scout are the way it should still be now. They were kind of the foundation of the way your life should be . . . A mission statement for each individual in life, to keep yourself physically fit and morally straight, to help other people at all times, to do my duty to God and my country; the list of attributes. All of this applies so greatly to today's life. How much better the world would be if people applied these things universally."

CHAPTER SIX

REGRET AND SUCCESS

Falling Short

THESE ARE THE STORIES of Scouts who fell short of the ultimate Scouting goal: Eagle. While Eagle is not the be-all and end-all of our existence, it still represents a goal in our youth that we might have attained if we had just applied ourselves a little harder, just stuck with it a little longer. It's an honor that, even today, heads still turn whenever someone lets it slip that they had been an Eagle Scout back in the day.   In talks with my fellow troop members, this seems to be a common regret among many. It seemed to bother Jerry Thetford the most. When I asked him if there was anything he could have done differently in his Scouting career, he said:

"Uh . . . (sigh) . . . made Eagle. That's the one thing that I didn't do that I look on back now. At the time, it didn't seem important. I mean I was still having a lot of fun with Scouts. I was still learning a lot of things with Scouts. I earned merit badges early on, and then after I turned 16, I got my own car, and those things just didn't seem as important to me. I got to Star, and I almost made it to Life, and then, I just kind of stopped working on them. I don't know why. I look back now, I wish I'd have; the other thing I wished I'd have been able to do which I didn't get to do, was to go to Philmont."

I reminded Jerry that *most* of us were guilty of not having gone all the way to Eagle, but his love of Scouting made him harbor this one slip. He did, however, manage to attend a

Jamboree with 42,000 other Scouts, at Camp Coeur d'Alene in Idaho where Bob Hope told jokes and Miss America sang—something most Scouts didn't get to enjoy.

I told Mr. Street about Jerry's sorrow at not attaining Eagle; he wrote to me concerning Jerry's Scout career, saying:

"I will have to say that Jerry was a good Scout even though he could have attained the Eagle rank as well as anyone else. The opportunity was there. I never had any trouble with him as he did what was asked of him."

Mark Dixon was more up front concerning his Scouting time; I asked him how far he got in his Scouting career, and his reply was "As best I recall, I was working on some of the merit badges, what have you, and I think I only got to First Class. I did get into Order of the Arrow; I don't think I ever progressed any further than First Class."

When I asked him why not, he said, "Probably laziness; I was having too good of a time. I enjoyed doing a lot of the merit badges, but around 1969 or 1970 my parents moved out of the area; I never got into another Scout troop."

When the DFW Airport came into existence, Mark's family sold their home to the Airport and moved to a farm north of McKinney, too far away for weekly Scouting meetings. The troop visited his parents' new home, however, and we had many camping trips on their land. Moving can take the wind out of a Scout's sails; he'd have to start all over with a new troop, new friends. Some kids can do it, but Mark had to get settled into a new high school.

To me, Chuck Wagner was almost a textbook example of a Boy Scout. Chuck was a Scout among Scouts. He demonstrated his leadership abilities at a younger age than most and became the Senior Patrol Leader at the age of 13.

Helpful, courteous, kind, he was all of these things, and he was involved in Scouting up to his ears. We discussed his situation. He never quit the Scouts; he loved it too much. His problem, as he explained it to me, was that he became involved with too many activities in the Scouting Programs:

"Let me first say that I have two regrets in my life— one is that I didn't make Eagle, and two is that I never saw Bing Crosby live in concert! But, as far as the Eagle goes, you kind of hit on it earlier . . . I got very involved in the Scouting program, very involved with the troop, all the way up to Senior Patrol Leader at a relatively young age . . . got into the O.A. and what they call the So'Tsoh Clan of Irving, which was the Order of the Arrow program of Irving. I got real involved with that. Mr. Street was very supportive of that. Mr. Street himself was a Vigil Honor member of the O.A., very very supportive of it. It just seemed like a natural progression . . . I'd gone to pretty much the summit of being a Troop Leader as the SPL . . . and so the O.A. kind of gave me a way to do other things and grow from there . . . and so I was real involved and became the Clan Chief of the O.A. clan and went on to become the Lodge Officer of Order Ward and Lodge Chief from there! Basically, you know, I think in my case, one of the things that happened was going from the next thing to the next thing, based upon what I got from the O.A. program, which was a life of cheerful service to others was something to be lauded and something to strive for. Once I got that bug, as they say, I was really no longer concerned at all with my own personal goals as far as rank, it really just meant very little to me. Merit badges were all well and good, but that seemed too self-focused, that seemed well like, another rank or something, I'd rather be out here planning a big fall fellowship and have a great time and do something where 300 or 400 other Scouts can have fun at;

or I'd like to organize the lodge in a different way that brings more people into it and gives more people the opportunity to help. So, I got so focused on all of that outside of myself that I completely neglected the rank. If I had to do it over again, I would have done the ranks before I got too involved there. I would still be involved, but I would have made sure I finished up my own personal stuff before I allowed myself to get too far involved in everything else."

Chuck Wagner volunteers to be the patient during a first-aid class; Jerry Thetford learning (at left).

I asked him if Mr. Street tried to let him know that time might run out for him one day, and he explained:

"Oh yes, definitely! To Mr. Street, becoming Eagle was very important to him, and he made sure that we all knew that it was very important to him. But, the other thing, to his credit, he made sure you understood that you weren't getting your Eagle for him, you were getting your Eagle for *you*. I've known throughout all the years in Scouting, I've known a whole lot of kids who have gotten their Eagle. They've done it for the wrong reasons. They've done it for Dad, they've done it for the Scoutmaster, and Mr. Street will tell you this, there are certain troops that are Eagle factories, I know you've heard those stories. I said that of course I had, and made mention that Troop 826 was no Eagle factory, to which Chuck added: No, Mr. Street wasn't going to allow it to be. Now, by the same token, Mr. Street wanted me to get my Eagle, he wanted me to get it because I'd worked for it and earned it, but in my particular case I chose to work for these other things instead of working for my Eagle, and I know that Mr. Street was disappointed in me for that. It is one thing that I regret, one of the two that I can think of in my life."

I told Chuck that if he only had two regrets in life, he was doing pretty good! I also suggested that we were young and beginning our adolescent years and that we shouldn't be too hard on ourselves for making mistakes. After all, that's where we get our experience, from making goofs! We could learn from them as well. Chuck agreed, saying:

"Absolutely! And that would be the only reason I mention it, if someone's reading this, if a young person's reading this, it is something I really stress, you will regret it if you don't go ahead and finish it off, if you don't meet that goal. I don't take pride in the fact that I'm not an Eagle or didn't get my Eagle . . . I don't beat myself up over it because there are a whole lot of people who never did, but given what I know now, I would really urge anyone who's in the program as a youth member to complete it, finish it, get that Eagle . . . it does so much for you in terms of your personal self-esteem when you complete that, and certainly, when you become an adult to have known that you're one of the few that did . . . and it helps later in life as you're associating with other people . . . as much as I do in Order of the Arrow, there's still an elite group of adults that are all ex-Eagle Scouts, former Eagle Scouts, the National Eagle Scout Association. They don't look down on people who weren't, but still, you do look up to the group there, that managed to attain that goal while they were all youth members, so, it's something to do, and I really urge any man that's in the program to go ahead and work hard and get that Eagle, you'll really be glad you did."

On the 826 Reunion Campout, Chuck Wagner displays a headdress made by Native American Bob Hooks, which Chuck wore for ceremonies with the Order of the Arrow.

As far as I know, Chuck has all the merit badges required for his Eagle badge. He's been involved in and done far more than any regular Scout has, but time just ran out for him while he was concentrating on other areas.

Chuck agreed that Mr. Street wasn't going to allow Troop 826 to be easy. In other words, there was to be some real work in earning awards and decorations. This reminded me of one episode back when I was around 12 or 13 years old. Once at the old Scout Hut, we had a visitor named George Alford. Mr. Alford was a highly favored Scout friend in the area, and Mr. Street just kind of turned the meeting over to him, which we kids loved. Mr. Alford told the troop that we were going to earn the Physical Fitness merit badge, and we were to get busy and start right now! So we Scouts all lined up and ran hurdles, did sit-ups, push-ups, standing broad jumps, running broad jumps, all while Mr. Alford watched and laughed and signed whatever form we put in front of him. We all liked Mr. Alford, especially when he helped us like this. The next week at school I was sore and stiff, being a little butterball, but happy in the knowledge that I had earned my Physical Fitness merit badge. My smile quickly disappeared at the next Scout meeting when Mr. Street stood up in front of the troop, taking a little "Physical Fitness" form and tore it up, saying "We don't earn a merit badge in one night. It takes weeks, maybe months to earn it the right way. You have to work at it and exercise and learn to take care of yourselves. It's not just a one-night event." Well, from that, I learned that work and responsibility were involved in earning merit badges—two concepts that were still foreign to me. Making rank wasn't going to be as easy as I had thought.

Mike Huebner expressed himself when asked about his not going all the way with the Scouting program:

"You know you have a question further down about quitting the Scouting program . . . that's one of my big regrets, is that I quit Scouts. I think one thing is, my Dad had a business, and I was working at that business on Saturdays and holidays and stuff, since I was in the seventh grade. I think I was just working. [Mike's father owned a machine shop.] Yeah . . . Dad still has it. I'm the vice president, actually; what I do now is I do accounting work for them. I think that's why I quit. I don't remember the other reasons why I quit. Yeah, you know looking back I wish I had stayed with it; it's funny when you're that age you have that attitude. Now I'd love to do it. I guess we could go be Scoutmasters."

Some in the troop did go back and serve in that capacity. Mike worked and learned a trade; he later taught physics at a local high school and is now studying to be a lawyer. His favorite merit badge was Rifle and Shotgun, and he still shoots in contests around the country. Chuck Wagner earned a Printing merit badge while in the Scouting program, which gave him a taste of the vocation that he would later go into. Jerry Thetford learned something about electronics, the vocation he wound up choosing.

Being exposed to different vocations and skills with the 21 merit badges required for Eagle is almost like a prep school for college. It offers a basic groundwork for the education and work that a young man will do for a living in order to support himself and his family in later years. The more a Scout learns when he's young, the more he'll be able to use when he's older. I believe that the merit badge system is superior to the public school system in this way; it's a hands-on method of learning practical skills and knowledge, a laboratory where the Scout can learn at his own speed, using his own skills, style, methods, and resources.

According to Jerry Thetford, Mr. Street spoke on the merit badges, the variety, telling the Scouts what the learning was all about:

Mike Huebner (r.) winning 2nd place in the first match of the Black Powder Cartridge Rifle Silhouette National Championships, 2009. Mike placed 2nd overall.

"Going through so many different merit badges, and the different activities that we did, I remember Mr. Street telling us one time, something like "It doesn't really matter what merit badges you take, whether you really like them or not, but sooner or later one of them hopefully will come along that will spark your interest as to what you want to do. So it exposes you to a lot of different things that you can learn and do, and it kind of helps you decide what you want to do later on in life." Now I did take an Electronics merit badge, and I ended up in electronics, so that may have sparked a bit of interest there, I don't really remember if it did."

When talking to Jerry about this, I mentioned that I had been to the BSA Headquarters Museum in Irving, to see the Norman

Rockwell paintings on exhibit. In doing so, I came across a merit badge display, complete with a shoulder sash with about 100 badges on it, and a wall covering with all sorts of badges, from the past to the present. There's no ending to what a Scout could learn if he had the desire!

These badges represent college or a preparation for college. A Scout who gets 21 of these is taking out a chunk of learning at a time, foreshadowing whether he would be able to earn a degree in college and not be overwhelmed by the aspect of it. Any Scout who does this knows he can handle higher education. He's succeeded in one area and this will transfer to another. He knows how to succeed, what it will cost him, and what he needs to do in order to complete his goal.

I'm not saying every Eagle badge recipient I've known is the president of a corporation, but in general, they seem to do better and go farther than the rest of us. The Scouts is also a family-, church-, school- and society-friendly organization. A young person who spends his time with them won't be getting himself into too much mischief.

My brother David explains why he didn't take Scouting all the way to the finish line; it was because he became involved with activities at the public school—MacArthur High School:

"I left the Scouts before my freshman year of high school because I was in Band. We had marching band rehearsals on Thursday nights, and that was the same night we had Scouts, and I just didn't think I could . . . I didn't know how I could. I enjoying band because there was girls! This was something we didn't have in Boy Scouts. There were some really cute girls there. I thought, "Well gosh, If I have to choose between Scouts and Band . . ." and it never occurred to me that I could do both. Honestly, I kind of wish I had tried to do that. And then you know we were going to have football games to go to on the weekends, and I thought, "How am I going to go camping if I have to go to these Football games?" So, I made the very mature decision to quit without really talking to anybody about it.

The only regret I have was that I didn't push harder to try to go for Eagle. You and I were talking one time and I mentioned that I was overwhelmed at the prospect of earning 21 merit badges, and I didn't think to break it down into segments. I just thought, "Oh my gosh that's too many, that's just too big a mountain!" Of course I've learned since then that you just take a job and you break it down into small pieces, and you accomplish each task in succession, and that gets you to your goal. Once again, I was a funny mixed bag. I was a really good student, but then I got intimidated by the prospect of working that hard and trying to earn that many badges, thinking that I could not measure up to guys like Ray Mahaffey or Jack Rankin. I just thought there's no way I could be equal to those guys. So they went on and did their thing, and I made my choice, and I just wish I had worked harder and had tried to figure out a way to stay in Scouts once high school started . . . because . . . a friend of mine in high school, who was in my class, his name was Harry Earl, he got his Eagle badge just before his senior year, and I admired him so much for that."

I had also made the poor choice to quit after David did. He was my older brother, and I was the copier. I didn't know how to do things on my own; so whatever David did, I usually wound up doing. Since David wasn't around, I didn't have anyone I felt I could copy, and school was pressing down on me. While David took off into academics, I was just trying to get by in the school setting. I graduated by the skin of my teeth, while David sailed through the land of academia, where I could not follow. I had to go to school; it was a 'have to' thing. I didn't 'get it,' and I made the choice to just survive. I let Scouting slip, and as I said earlier, finally woke up to what a great program Scouting was years later. David said:

"Well, everybody wakes up at different points in their life, when they realize "Oh gosh . . . so that's what it was all about!" Lights go off in guy's heads at different points in their lives. Some guys like . . . Jack Rankin was always a very driven individual. He just knew what he wanted to do and he just went after it."

It's not something I punish myself for; it's just that I wish I had a better grasp on things. So here I am, an adult, writing on the benefits of the Scouting program, what an effect Troop 826 had on my life and on the lives of others. I ask myself: "Who am I, someone who didn't finish what he started, to tell others about the benefits?" The only satisfactory answer I can come up with is that a person doesn't have to be perfect to tell the truth. I don't have to be an Eagle Scout to share the success stories I've witnessed where others finished the course. I wasn't an Eagle, but hopefully I was a good Scout. Hopefully I am and can continue to be a good man, which is one of the many goals of Scouting.

Success

I used to see Mr. Street a lot while at the local spa, er, gym. We both had memberships at the Bally's Spa, and while sitting around in the steam room we would talk about and remember the days of Scouting. Mr. Street would keep me up to date on many of the Scouts who had been in the troop during my time. I was glad to listen and was eager to hear about them. After he told me about many of the boys who had become successful men, I began to notice a pattern, which wasn't really hard to figure out. I said to Mr. Street, "You know, it seems to me that many of the boys who went far in the Scouts also went far with their chosen careers." Mr. Street agreed. It had become pretty obvious that the boys who made it high in the Scouting ranks also went on to have successful or colorful careers. These were the boys who learned how to set goals and keep at it. These learned traits served them well later in a competitive world.

As an example, I've thought about those people in my own family . . . my younger brother and my older cousin both earned 20 merit badges. They were both within one merit badge and project of becoming an Eagle Scout, and then they both lost interest and dropped out. I don't know if this has haunted them in later years; maybe it does. I haven't broached the subject with them. However, both of these Scouts went on to complete their education and become engineers. They have done well for themselves in their adult careers. I'm proud of them both; they're good, helpful, and productive.

Success is something this Scout always dreamed of, and yet it seems to somehow slip away. Success, like responsibility, turned out to be another slippery concept. I've learned to be content with what I've done and what I have; I've had to! In one sense I've been a success—I've successfully managed to keep out of jail. But that could change at any time. I don't think a Scout is required to be successful, but to be at his best—to strive to be a solution, not part of the problem.

A few years back, I read a story about the Wright brothers. Before they invented the airplane, they asked their father, a minister, how hard a person should work. Their father answered, "A person should work hard enough so he won't be a burden on others." Well, the two Wright brothers did this and then some, and in doing so, created a new travel industry for the world.

We're all not equipped the same, but whatever we do in life should be, as the Bible puts it, for the glory of God and for the help of man. Having these as his aim, the Scout will be well on his way to doing his best.

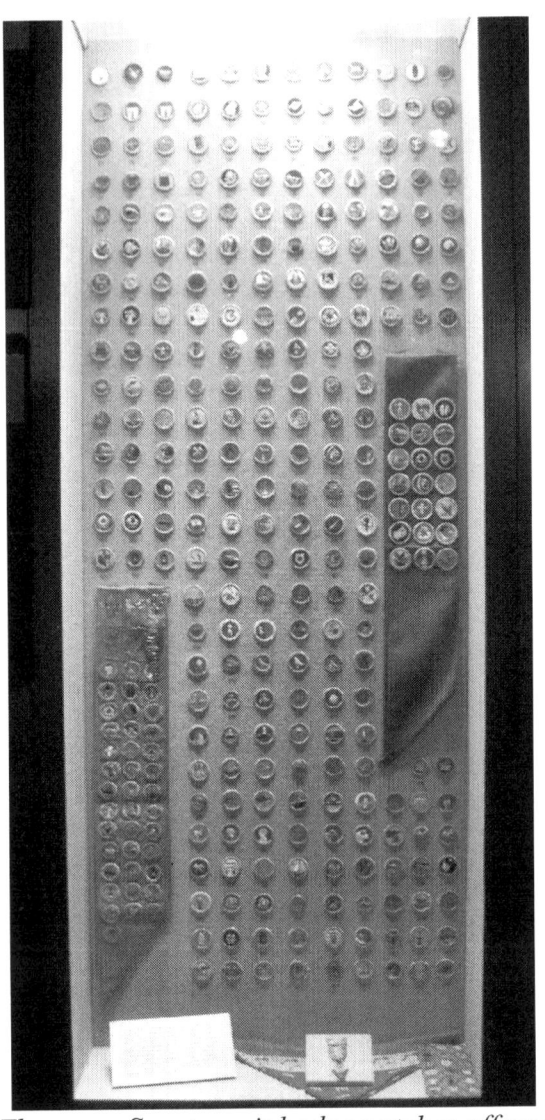

*The many Scout merit badge patches offered
over the years from a display at the
National Boy Scouts of America Headquarters,
Boy Scout Museum in Irving, Texas*

CHAPTER SEVEN

CAMPOUTS AND OTHER ADVENTURES

The First Campout

ONE THING MOST of the Troop 826 Scouts remember was their first time away from home on a real Boy Scout campout; out in the woods, man against nature, into survival territory. They packed up their sleeping rolls, cooking gear, backpacks, tents, utensils, Scout books, and met over at Mr. Street's house where we would all depart for the wilderness. Sometimes just getting to the camping area was an adventure in itself. Once, we stopped to view a small food factory along the way. I guess we were supposed to see and learn how a business operated.

Things don't work in the country like they do in the city. There's no heating or air-conditioning, no beds, no Mother to cook, no Father to tell us what to do next, no television, and no telephones. All we had was a campfire to cook on and the Scoutmaster and other adult supervision to keep us out of trouble and to tell us our job(s) for the weekend. Most of us weren't used to taking orders from anyone outside of the family or classroom. Here we had to learn teamwork and cooperation, or else it wasn't going to be an easy time.

Mark Dixon remembered clearly the situations on his first campout:

"The first campout I even went on, I remember it like it was yesterday—being a new kid in Scouts and not knowing anything about camping. All the troop really had at the time were pup tents, two man pup tents. I remember the first campout. When we got to the campsite, it may have been 35 or 40 degrees outside. We set up the tents. Seems like it was in East Texas where we camped out, and I remember there was a railroad track very close to where the campsite was. As a matter of fact, we used to go up and put pennies and quarters and nickels on the track, the train would come through, and we'd go back up and find our squished coins, kind of a neat deal. But I also remember on that first campout I went on, it rained that evening. I remember somebody telling me "Don't touch the inside of a tent." Well you know that's an invitation; so in the process, I remember reaching up and touching the inside of the tent! The next morning I woke up and there was an icicle hanging down over me, on the inside. The temperature had gotten pretty cold that night; seems like it got down in the 20s, in the low 20s. I remember thinking, "What am I doing here?" By the time I finally got out of my sleeping bag, looking outside the tent, and Mr. Street had the biggest, blazing fire that you could ever imagine, and I mean, it was sooo good to back up to that nice big warm fire. I remember food never tasting better in a situation like that; milk never tasted better. The air was so crisp; it was one of those memories that endeared camping out. Sometimes the best things come from the more adverse conditions that you're in. It was one of those things. I was hooked from that point on. If I've endured the toughest campout that I've ever imagined, all the rest of them were like gravy. But it was great."

My brother David spoke of his first campout, which happened at a time when he was preparing to join Troop 826. He was a purist and had high hopes when it came to finding honorable youth, a better people, a noble tribe:

"Well, you know, like I said, there's a lot of memories. I think back to my first campout experience and that was when I was still in Cub Scouts. I was a Webelos Scout. I wasn't quite old enough to join the Scouts yet as a Tenderfoot, so I was 10 years old. I went on a campout with the Eagle Patrol: Mike Quine, Ray Mahaffey, Alvin Brown I believe, possibly even Mark Dixon. I think Mr. Mahaffey and Mr. Nelson took us out. I was 10 years old, so that would have been 1965. Good grief! The fall or winter of 1965, I went on my first camping trip. I didn't have a sleeping bag, Mama had gotten a tarp and pinned blankets on the inside of it, and so I didn't have a sleeping bag per say, I had a sleeping roll. She worked hard and got me some food pulled together. I didn't have a Boy Scout uniform; I had a Cub Scout uniform. So I took it, and I remember, Mike Quine took me aside and said, "You know, David, the guys on this campout, they don't act like the boys you look at in the *Boy Scout Manual,* they don't act like what you see in *Boy's Life Magazine.*" I guess I was kind of idealistic and starry eyed, "You mean they're not perky little robot guys that they always use as the uber examples in the books and all?" So I remember being disappointed in the guys, but I think that I liked the guys; and so I think that maybe that taught me that every single human being is fallible and yet likeable. We're all a mixed bag of good and bad, but I think 95 to 98 percent of the folks that are out there are good people and worthy of love and respect; and so I kind of picked that up, too."

Acceptance: a good lesson to learn while young. David's nickname in the Troop was 'Biscuit.' I asked him how he managed to get stuck with that moniker. He alluded to the Pillsbury Doughboy and said that since he was kind of roly-poly when young, and 'Bennett' sounded similar to 'Biscuit,' it was just too easy to make the connection.

Food was an important part in the survival of camping, especially for novices. I found the easiest method was a hotdog on a coat hanger. You stick it on, cook it, eat it, no plates, no mess, no clean up. Once Mama taught me how to cook fried chicken, however, there was plenty to clean up around the campfire after that.

Chuck Wager and Jerry Thetford tell of their first campout experiences, both of which involved food mishaps. Chuck learned something the hard way, not because he wasn't eager to learn, but because he wasn't experienced. When he relayed this story to me, I mentioned that the "Be Prepared" slogan hadn't soaked in yet; Chuck agreed:

"That's true. No, I was unclear on the concept, as they say. As I recall, I think I had been in the troop for a month or less, when I was at the Troop meetings. I think Steve Fellows was the Senior Patrol Leader at that point. They were talking about the campout, and they were talking about the meals, where it wouldn't be patrol-cooked meals. They would be individual meals, and everybody had to bring their own food. I guess being eleven and stupid, it never occurred to me that . . . what could I bring that didn't require refrigeration? I didn't have an ice chest and didn't even think you were *allowed* to bring ice chests; so my rations for the weekend consisted primarily of Pop-Tarts, white frosted doughnuts, and a few candy bars. I did learn that you could glaze white frosted doughnuts by putting them on a stick and holding them over a fire. It was pretty awful and embarrassing, because you know I showed up there and everybody showed up bringing ice chests all over the place ... they're eating like kings, and I'm sitting there with my toasted doughnuts. And as I recall, either Mr. Street or somebody took pity on me during the weekend. I know I had a decent meal.

Somebody shared something with me. It was an interesting opening experience."

Jerry Thetford tells of a similar hard case on his first campout, not because of him, but because of his fellow patrol members:

"I remember my very first campout. We had met the week before to decide what we're all going to take out camping with us and what we were going to eat when we were there. For some reason, there were only 3 or 4 in our patrol; it wasn't a big patrol. When I got there Friday night, no one else showed up in our patrol, I was there by myself. I had $5 on me, because that's how much we were supposed to pay for food that weekend. And so, on the way up there, we stopped, and I got some hotdogs and some buns in hopes that would get me through the weekend. Mr. Street kind of saw what was happening, so he put me in a different patrol, he made sure I had plenty of food to eat, you know he was always looking out for the boys. One thing I'll never forget was, seems like he would always make desert, he'd make a kind of a cobbler. And it seemed like he'd usually make two. Of course there was usually only him and Mr. Johnson out there, and there's no way they're going to be able to eat two cobblers or even a full cobbler for the most part. So after us eating cold sandwiches or burnt hotdogs or spaghetti that didn't get cooked all the way, we always knew that Mr. Street would have leftovers. We would always kind of hang around his campsite as closely as possible. We knew as soon as he said,

"I did learn that you could glaze white frosted doughnuts by putting them on a stick and holding them over a fire."

"I've got some leftovers!" We were hightailing it to his camp to get some cherry cobbler or whatever it might have been. We'd be eating hotdogs or attempt to make hamburgers, while Mr. Street was having fried chicken, mashed potatoes, corn on the cob. And we figured that if he can do that, we can too, and eventually we learned how to do that. I remember when I first got into Scouting as a leader. I remember those times when Mr. Street was eating really good food, and we were eating hotdogs, and so I got involved in the troop. And sure enough, on our first campout, it hadn't changed. They were still eating hotdogs; they were still burning their hamburgers; and I had steak that night, baked potatoes. I boiled some water and had some corn on the cob. Eventually the boys started thinking,

"Hey man, it's not this hard to cook this." And they'd come and ask me how to cook something, and that was one of the times I felt fulfilled as a Scout leader, because I remember these are the things Mr. Street taught me, and these are the things I'm hopefully passing on to them."

Chuck Wagner (l.) and Jerry Thetford (r.) cooking for the rest of us at the Troop 826 Reunion Campout in 2006

Mr. Street taught by example here, and was known for his cooking skills, especially with the Dutch oven. He wrote me once to tell me about it:

"I too remember the times that boys brought wrong camp food, and for that reason, I would bring some extras that I shared when I cooked. The boys soon learned from their mistake of not planning for a good meal. I think that the first meal a boy learned to cook was the foil cooking. It was an easy and fast meal to prepare. Just have a good bed of coals to cook. Not many missed out getting some of my cobblers."

He rescued many a scout from scarce or burnt food . . . and his cooking was so good that even the adult supervision stood around hoping for leftovers!

My first campout was summer camp at BSA Camp Wisdom, so I didn't have to survive on my own cooking. I did manage to fall into a cooking class there, though, learning to get something right in aluminum foil.

It's funny, though; Mr. Street didn't allow soda pops at 826 campouts. I asked him about that later on, and he said it caused too much mess, whenever one of the Scouts opened a can it would spray everything everywhere, which of course the kids thought was funny but created clean-up work. Mr. Street usually had a good reason for his requirements on campouts. He doesn't like all the electronic gadgets that kids have now; he'd like for them to turn the phones off and leave the toys at home. He also doesn't like the fact that Scouts need air conditioning in the camp cafeterias. We sure didn't! We drank lots of water and learned to sweat like men.

That first campout can be hard at times—when you're tired or out of your routine, you just can't go back to your house for a nap; you have to keep going, to keep up with the other Scouts. With a full day's activity, there's no trouble sleeping at night. I cried at my first campout. I didn't understand the older boys who were trying to be my boss. I've seen other scouts cry also, for really no reason except that they were tired or felt out of place. After we realized that everything was going to be all right, and that we had found something we could do, that we found a niche, camping out became the adventure it was supposed to be—surviving in the wild, with hotdogs and Pop-Tarts.

Other Adventures

I was talking with Mike Huebner about his favorite Scouting adventures, and he had this to share:

"Well, I remember . . . once we went camping at Camp Texoma, and there was like a cliff, and we were climbing it or at least I was climbing it, and I found mortar shells, several of them. We took them down, and I showed them to Mr. Street, or somebody. It might have been Mr. Quine, and I guess we were at a state park because they took them to the state park or ranger's station. Come to find out, they had used that cliff during WWII for mortar practice. It might have been during the Korean War. . . . They might be in the ranger's station now. I ought to go up there and look and say, "I found those!""

Jerry Thetford was fortunate enough to attend the National Boy Scout Jamboree in 1973 at Coeur d'Alene State Park on Lake Coeur d'Alene in Idaho, and he told me about the experience:

"I do remember him [Bob Hope] at that Boy Scout Jamboree. We had this one big huge arena where all the Scouts could meet. At the time, we were only supposed to have 25,000 boys at that camp. That year they were supposed to have two camps, one in Idaho and one in Pennsylvania. Well, the one in Pennsylvania basically got flooded out. So a lot of those Scouts ended up coming to Idaho. When it was all said and done we had over 42,000 Boy Scouts. We had this one arena, kind of built out of a mountainside with a little stage at the bottom, and

Bob Hope came out one night, told jokes, just did what he normally does. There was something different that happened each night. One night I remember they had Miss America who came out and got to see all the Scouts, and we were like "Oooo, Miss America, she's so hot." I remember one of the things, the one thing that really sticks out in my mind, and I believe it was the last time we all had a big meeting there. When we walked into the arena, they handed everyone a candle, a little candle that you'd put on the top of a cake to blow out. They told us all not to light them, just to wait. So . . . it was late afternoon, early evening, the sun was starting to go down. We all took our places on the side of the hill. We were waiting. The thing got started. Eventually it got dark, and they talked about how important a single idea is, and that one person can change the world, and you can make a difference just by yourself, and he was going to use this candle to demonstrate that. So what this guy did was, he lit his candle, and then he lit some candles on the first row, and then they started lighting people's candles behind them, and behind them, and behind them, and before you know it there were 42,000 candles lit up at one time. The stadium was completely lit! I'll never forget how cool that was to have 42,000 candles lit up at the same time from a single candle."

Jerry Thetford, circa 1972

CHAPTER EIGHT

TO DO MY BEST

The Eagles

THIS SECTION IS DEDICATED to the hardest-working and most serious-minded Scouts of Troop 826, the Eagle Scouts. They were (in the order in which they were awarded the honor) Jack Rankin, Duane Tarver, Ray Mahaffey Jr., Mike Quine, and Steve Rackley.

I wanted to know what made these Scouts tick. I wanted to know their philosophies concerning the Scouting program and beyond. I was curious about how life turned out for them. When I did find out, it was no surprise to see they were all married, family men (one of whom is a grandfather), and successful in their vocational endeavors. All of the Eagles were grateful to the Scouting program for what it meant to them, and they agreed that the Boy Scouts of America had nothing to apologize for. I interviewed them all separately, except for Ray Mahaffey. Sadly, Ray was involved in a fatal car accident in 1982. I did manage to speak with his parents, and his story follows this chapter.

I found Jack Rankin on the Internet. His CPA business is in the city of Bedford, and I drove over to visit with him in August of 2008. Jack Rankin was the first Eagle of Troop 826. He was also in the first generation of Scouts. He grew up scouting. Jack became one of the leaders of the troop, and many of the younger Scouts viewed him as an adult. His father, Calvin Johnson worked in the background and was happy to be of assistance to any Scout who needed help, was one of the regular volunteers active in the troop. Jack Rankin told me,

"The Boy Scouts of America taught me that nothing comes easy in life. There is a direct relationship between what you get out of life and what you put into it. I am most definitely a better man because of Scouting. It made me tough. It gave me an appreciation for the outdoors and wildlife. It made me appreciate things. It's made me humble and hopefully given me more compassion for mankind than I would have otherwise had. My hat goes off to all the volunteers in scouting that are trying to make a difference! Without them, there would not be a Scouting program. Viva the Boy Scouts of America!"

Jack Rankin, senior portrait, MacArthur High School, 1972.

I questioned Duane Tarver over the e-mail in July of 2008. He was also one of the earlier Scouts. He was friends with my brother David and had this manner about him that just somehow always made me laugh; his mind was always active. Duane spent probably 80 percent of his Scouting days with Troop 826, and later transferred to another troop where he received his Eagle badge. But because he grew up and did most of his Scouting with us, he's included here with the other Eagles. Duane spent 20 years in the Navy with nuclear submarines, and now works for the federal government again. When I asked him about his time in Scouts, Duane said,

Duane Tarver, senior portrait, MacArthur High School, 1972.

"The Scouts taught me several things. One of the most important is what you can accomplish as a group. Second is what you can accomplish as an individual. In my life, Scouting helped me learn that it is best sometimes not to be 'cool' but hold to your personal values and not worry so much about what others think of you. The values they taught us still hold true today. They taught me discipline, teamwork, how to sustain a drive to goals, friendship, and how to survive in a world that is constantly changing."

I caught up with Mike Quine and Steve Rackley at our Sid Richardson Troop 826 Reunion Campout in September of 2006. If their answers seem shorter than the other two Scouts, it's because I failed to put new batteries in my tape recorder. I furiously wrote their answers on paper. They were questioned hours apart. Mike Quine was also friends with David, which is how I first met Mike and became good childhood friends with his little brother Kevin. Mike is gifted in the areas of music, art, and organizing. Mike made us younger Scouts laugh. We wished we had his creativity. When I asked Mike what he thought the Scouts taught him and what he took with him that helped him in life, he said:

"They taught me to be a good person, what was right, and that I could be self-sufficient. There was a quote I learned later, Calvin Coolidge said it, about persistence: to never give up. And I carried that through my Scouting career and life. Nothing will take you further than persistence. I hope that in some way I have had or will have the opportunity to be the kind of role model that Mr. Street was for all of us. I look back at those times, those golden years, as some of the best in my life. I also

Rank and Awards display, belonging to
Eagle Scout Michael Quine,
a gift from his wife Jane.

see the empty spaces that Ray Mahaffey, Mark Null and my brother Kevin have left in my later years. So I would say to everyone, take time to make a difference when you can, make a memory for someone to keep, take the point and lead the way. Live as an eagle; it's never too late."

Mike Quine at his Eagle Award ceremony, receiving the Scout Handshake from Scoutmaster Warren Street. Mike's parents, Hilton Quine and Nell Welborn, were also present.

Steve Rackley was a member after I had arrived and left. He's with the third generation of Scouts of Troop 826. I was fortunate enough to meet Steve at the Reunion Campout. He's the kind of person who's easy to be friends with. It was easy to see how he became an Eagle Scout. As an Eagle Scout, he said he had been a "marked man," a phrase used in his Eagle Ceremony, and it gave him an edge over the competition when he applied for his present vocation as a consultant, since leadership was what his employers were looking for. I asked Steve what he thought the Scouts taught him and what he took with him that helped him in life, he said:

Steve Rackley at his Eagle Ceremony, 1978.

"To do what you say you're gonna do, to follow through, to make a commitment. The leadership skills I learned! Scouting kept me balanced in being of service to others, thinking about others. It's not all feats. I was involved in the OA (Order of the Arrow), and they taught me it's important to serve others. They gave me direction in my life. I would literally like to thank all the adults involved with my scouting. Mr. Street, Mr. Johnson, Mr. White, the Assistant Scoutmasters, the committee members who sacrificed time to keep things running smoothly and who helped to keep me out of trouble when I was a kid. Other than my father, Warren Street had the biggest impact on making me the adult I am today."

On the Path to Success

I have a friend named David Couric. A few years back, he and I met at a local Chinese restaurant for an early supper and to catch up on college days. The evening rush had not yet arrived to crowd the place, so we were the only customers in the family-owned shop. As we sat and enjoyed the oriental decorations, we noticed a little boy, probably about 9 or 10 years old, and his mother sitting at one of the tables near the kitchen door. We knew the lady was the wife of the owner; the little boy was their son. He had a schoolbook and pencil and pad in front of him. His mother was seated across the table, leaning forward to hear what he was reading to her. It was evident he was working on mathematics, and she was helping him. She would explain and correct him from time and time, and with that he would go back to his reading and working on his figures.

David said, "That's why they're whipping us," meaning that the Asian students in our school system were leaving Anglo-American children behind in the educational dust. I knew this to be true just by seeing area high school honor graduates in the newspaper. Where Jones and Smith used to be, now there were Chen and Nguyen. There's nothing racial here; this is just a sociological/societal observation. More power to them! This restaurant owner's wife was making sure that her son would have a fighting chance in the scholastic world.

I tell about this little scene because it illustrates what a few of the Eagle Scouts had in common: involved parents. Mr. Mahaffey (Ray Mahaffey Jr.'s father) and Mr. Johnson (Jack

Rankin's adoptive father) were constant volunteers to the troop and went with us on many campouts. I never saw them interfere with anything the Scouts or Mr. Street did. They were there in a supportive fashion. I'm sure they also encouraged and helped their sons in working their way toward the Eagle badge. Mr. Quine, Mike's dad, was also known to the Scout troop, and I found one photo where he attended a summer camp with the boys. How many fathers would give up a week's vacation to be with a group of Scouts? That's three of the five Eagle Scouts I've interviewed whose fathers were involved to the point of my knowing who they were. I also had met Mr. Tarver, who was supporting a family of six, as my father was. I couldn't fault him or my father for staying at home, wanting to sleep in their own beds after working long and hard to feed and keep us. I didn't know Mr. Rackley, Steve's father, but it appears that he was also supportive of his son, as was his mother.

Jack told me that he lived in the same neighborhood as Mr. Street; in fact, he lived just a few houses away. He was good friends with Rodney Street, and whenever he wanted to know something about the Scout program, he'd just take a little walk and talk to Scoutmaster Street about it. Mike did the same. He said that Mr. Street was there for him and helped him when he came back to Scouting.

It doesn't take a genius to know that the American family isn't exactly what the Cleavers were on *Leave It to Beaver* or the Andersons from the *Father Knows Best* television shows. In those programs the head of the house was a man who had a steady job and supported and loved his family, always had time for each child, and there was no fighting at any time, except between siblings. In reality, families in our country have a hard time living up to such high ideals, and it's depressing to try to be steady and yet fall short. If a boy can find a man to relate to, to plug in with, to get guidance from, and be a friend with, he may stand a chance in life. A mother will be supportive almost by her very nature, but a man can help a boy become productive, and as a byproduct, perhaps find a little happiness.

These Eagle Scouts were helped by men, mostly, and succeeded early, clearing a path for more success later on. They knew how to succeed. Sure, the definition of success is different from person to person, but these boys had done it once and learned from that success how to do it again.

CHAPTER NINE

ABSENT FRIENDS

The Missing Eagle

RAY MAHAFFEY JR. was more than an Eagle Scout to Troop 826. Before achieving that rank, he was the Senior Patrol Leader for the boys working closely with Jack Rankin, the Assistant SPL. Ray Jr.'s span of Scouting lasted from 1965 until he received his Eagle badge in 1971. Many Scouts came and went during that time; Ray was a constant.

The reason for this section is because Ray meant something to us boys. He was a friend and peer, but because of his presence in the Scouting program, we almost thought of him as one of the adult leaders. He liked to have fun with us, but he also knew and learned when to draw the line and to start acting responsibly. That is why so few of us became leaders; we liked to have fun all the time.

I spoke with Ray's parents, Ray Sr. and Lois Mahaffey, in the same house where they raised Ray Jr. and his two sisters, Betty and Patty, years ago. The Mahaffeys, now in their eighties, are grateful for the time Ray had in the Scouts and for what the program meant to him. He had a short and bright life; and as Mark Dixon put it: ". . . of all the guys of the troop that I was fond of, Ray Mahaffey had a special place in all of our hearts."

Ray Mahaffey Jr., born 1954, passed away in 1982 at the age of 28 because of a traffic accident. He became an Eagle Scout at 17, a husband at 19, marrying Judy George, and a father a few years later to daughter Carrie. Ray went to a

Technical Training school for Electronics and was employed with Microwave Communications Incorporated (MCI) as a linesman before he graduated. Ray and his family moved and settled in the city of Graham, Texas, some 120 miles northwest of Irving. Carrie was five when Ray died, so she never really got to know him while growing up. She has heard a lot about him from the Scouts in later years, what we thought and felt about him; this means a lot to her.

Ray Mahaffey Jr. at his Eagle Ceremony

Ray wanted to play sports when he was younger, but a stomach condition prevented him from being physically active until he had an operation for it in the fifth grade. He used to endure pain as a young boy until his condition was finally treated. While recovering, his fifth-grade teacher from A.S. Johnston Elementary, Mrs. Robinson, would drop by after school to bring Ray his lessons and keep him up to date so that he didn't fall too far behind his classmates.

We (the younger Scouts) would go to Ray first when we had questions or wanted permission to do something that we knew the adults would say "no" to. So we'd go to Ray, and many times he'd say "yes." He was a listener. Mrs. Mahaffey told me a story about Chuck Wagner asking to speak to her at Ray's funeral. She said,

"Well, he [Chuck] came up to the car after the funeral. We were waiting for everybody else to get into their cars, and he asked if he could talk to me. He said there was one thing he wanted me to know, that no matter what he needed to know, he would go to Ray, and Ray would stop whatever he was doing and help him.

I hoped some of that came from me, I would like to think, because Ray would come home kind of teary eyed and crying sometimes when he didn't get any help at a Scout meeting. And I would say, "You remember this whenever you get to the top and somebody else is at the bottom. You help whoever asks you; that's part of the Scout Creed, you know."

Chuck said that meant more to him than anything, because he'd been discouraged when he couldn't find help. He may have been on the verge of dropping out, and then Ray began helping him.

A few years later, Chuck would take over the responsibility of being the Senior Patrol Leader, and he spoke about Ray saying:

"Ray Mahaffey, you know, was just another tremendous example. I've mentioned before that as I would go on later in Scouting, it was very often when I was in a position of responsibility or have some obligation to meet, I would stop and think, "How would Ray Mahaffey handle this?" I'd always want to make sure. I knew if I was following his lead or his example that there was no way I'd be off the mark. He had a very, very strong influence on me."

When I asked Mrs. Mahaffey if Ray had ever been in the National Honor Society or any other high-achiever's club, she said:

Lois Mahaffey, Ray Mahaffey Jr., and Ray Mahaffey Sr.
at Ray's Eagle ceremony

No, I'll tell you what he was. He was either an "A" student or a "C" student. A teacher said, "How do you know that?" and I said, "Because if he got an "A," he knows it; he doesn't have any problem with it. And if he got a "C," he earned every bit of it believe me!

Strangely enough, it was kind of reassuring to hear that Ray wasn't in academia. It gives a hope for the rest of us; a person doesn't have to be Einstein to make it to the top. Ray's tenacity and dedication put him ahead of his peers in the Scouting program. Somewhere along the line he had learned the concepts of discipline and hard work.

Mr. Mahaffey attended one of our Troop 826 Reunion Parties, Mr. Street's 80th birthday in 2003. At the party, we all visited with Mr. Street and got caught up with each other, and at one point, there were about five Scouts gathered in the kitchen. We were standing around talking about campouts, remembering people who weren't there, and Mr. Mahaffey walked in and joined the conversation. During this time, one of the Scouts said to him how much Ray had meant to him with his time in Scouts and how sorry he was to hear of Ray's accident, even though 20 years had already passed. All of us joined in telling Mr. Mahaffey what Ray meant to us. We may have embarrassed Mr. Mahaffey a bit, but I know he was glad to hear it. I don't think he and Mrs. Mahaffey knew just how much Ray meant and was appreciated by the Scouts of the troop. He was an example to us, a straight arrow. We trusted Ray, and didn't have to wonder if he would be unstable, as many young people could be.

Mr. Mahaffey said that Ray's Eagle project involved the Space Program. Ray was in Scouts when the Astronauts landed on the moon, and all of a sudden, kids everywhere were interested. According to Mr. Mahaffey:

"He organized a bus trip from here to NASA in Houston. This was out at Ellington Field. The headquarters for NASA was pretty much near Galveston. He had a busload of Scouts on this trip. All of this interest led toward the development of an Air/Space merit badge."

Monte Pipes, Mike Quine, and Ray Mahaffey Jr. during their 50-mile ride for the Cycling merit badge.

The Mahaffeys said that Ray was proud of the work he put in on his Cycling merit badge. They told me about the 50-mile round-trip that he and Mike Quine and Monte Pipes took to Monte's grandparents' house in the country and how Ray spoke of it often. This was before all the bicycles sold were ten-speeds.

When asked if Ray had a favorite merit badge, Mr. Mahaffey said, "I really don't think so. I know he enjoyed working on all of them. The peculiar thing of it was that he took his own time. He didn't rush to get it done by the time he was 12. He was about 18 when he got it, and he just took his own time, and it worked out very well for him."

I told the Mahaffeys one story about Ray, which they'd never heard. Once on a campout, we had a little free time, so we got away from the adult area of the camp and found a field where we started playing a game of touch football. I was about 12 years old then, so many of the players were older and bigger, but that was okay since nobody was going to get tackled or hurt. Anyhow, during the game, I messed up one play and got knocked flat from behind by an older member on my team. No adults were around to coach or referee, so of course most kids looked the other way since I really did miss that play. While I'm on the ground, trying to gather my senses, I heard Ray Mahaffey, who was on the *other team* coming across the line of scrimmage onto *our* side to get in the face of the Scout who knocked me flat. I heard Ray chewing this fellow out and setting him straight, and the other fellow trying to justify himself, and Ray finally saying, "I don't care *what* he did, you don't knock people around whenever you feel like it! This is touch football; play the game right. What's wrong with you?!"

Now Ray wasn't a very big fellow, but he had a lot of respect from the Scouts, so whatever he said went. I didn't play anymore that day, but Ray stood a little taller in my eyes after that, sticking up for me the way he had.

A month after Ray passed away, Mr. & Mrs. Mahaffey participated in a ceremony commemorating Ray's life, at A.S. Johnston Elementary—Ray's school and the same place we held our early troop meetings. They planted a tree in Ray's honor, and their minister officiated. Mrs. Robinson, Ray's fifth-grade teacher, didn't know anything about the dedication.

She was surprised when someone brought a corsage for her to her classroom before the service. Mrs. Mahaffey said:

"They had Ray Jr.'s fifth-grade class that he was in. They were there. And they had Jennifer, Betty's [Ray's sister] oldest . . . and they had Jeff, her youngest. They invited his class because he of course knew about Ray Jr.'s death, you know, and they had those two classes out there. And those little kids were so sweet, and they were just whispering about that tree, you know. Mr. Mahaffey remarked, "One little girl came up to Lois and said, 'He must have been a nice little boy.'" Mrs. Mahaffey finished, " . . . and I said, 'He was the best,' and he was as far as I was concerned."

When interviewing Jerry Thetford for this record, I drove to Azle, Texas. After speaking to Jerry, it occurred to me that I was almost halfway to Graham so why don't I just drive on out there? I got in the van trying to remember the direction from the Mahaffeys, to stay on the highway and at the fork, take a left at the Dairy Queen.

I found Pioneer Cemetery with no trouble but then noticed the thousands of headstones. I was lost until I recalled that the Mahaffeys' telephone number was saved in my cell phone. Mrs. Mahaffey told me to go to the center, then to look south, and that Ray's headstone was cut from red rock. With these instructions, it was easy to find Ray Jr.'s resting place. His tombstone read ". . . to live is Christ; to die is gain." For a few moments that afternoon I was able to visit and thank Ray for the troop and for being the kind of person he was and for his helping to make Troop 826 what it was.

Ray Mahaffey Jr. and Monte Pipes, circa 1965.

Remembering Friends

Once a person has been in Scouts and made friends, Scouting never really ends. Whenever he meets a former troop member, it's a Scouting reunion for both of them. It's also painful when a member leaves us behind.

When Kevin Quine passed away suddenly at age 40, all the memories of our friendship came rushing back to me, it was almost overwhelming. I saw his obituary while at work. It was too much, and I broke down and cried. All our adventures came to mind: Once we had been playing around a construction site (where we shouldn't have been), my legs were caught and crushed by heavy lumber and it was Kevin who ran to get help. Another time I had chased Kevin out of our house, scaring him with my plastic Frankenstein and Wolf Man models. We both followed our brothers into Scouting and had many other fun adventures, skits, and exploring. The first person I went to after work was our Scoutmaster, Mr. Street, who already knew about Kevin passing away. I wouldn't be able to visit Kevin now and check up on him, find out how he was doing, remember with him; we were completely cut off.

I asked Chuck Wagner about his relationship with Kevin, and he told me,

"Kevin impressed me in so many ways, but primarily it was the fearlessness; he was one of those people, he would try anything. . . . the guy was a natural born engineer, a mechanical engineer. He could build anything. It was just amazing. That's a skill set I don't possess. I'm really in awe of that when I see somebody who can do it, but especially at that young age. The shelter that he built on the side of the hill at Texoma, it was just incredible."

Kevin Quine

When I told Chuck that I thought that was a Quine family characteristic—once they focus on something, they'll get it done. Chuck agreed with me saying,

"I think you're right. That's one of the things I recall about Kevin. Hopefully one of the positive influences that he had on me was that he had an unquestioning belief that he could do anything he wanted to do... that's such a great example to see, and if it weren't for a program like Scouting, I don't know that as a kid you'll get the opportunity to meet so many people that have that about them. I'm hopeful there was something about me that rubbed off on some other kid. The whole program gives you an opportunity to see and meet other people and get to know them, and hopefully to take away from those experiences and those friendships some parts of one another as you build your own character. That's what I recall from Kevin was primarily just his unshaken belief that he could do anything, and that's really helped me a lot as I've grown older."

Mike Quine experienced the loss of his brother, plus years earlier the same thing when he heard about Mark Null, one of the older Scouts who had been his close friend. He remembered:

"I spent weekends at Mark's house swimming in the pool trying to perfect our cannonball and can opener dives. It seems like as soon as we were through swimming his mom always had a big batch of hot homemade chocolate chip cookies coming out of the oven with ice cold milk to wash them down. It just didn't get much better than that. Mark and I attended the same church in Dallas, Central Christian. We went to church camp one year and it was there, for the first and only time, that we nearly came to blows. We were fists up and ready to go. I don't remember what started the whole thing but it was over quickly and we were best friends again the next day. Before high school, Mark's family moved to Corpus Christi. We eventually lost touch and it was many years later when I got the call that Mark had died. I had to play that night but after the gig when I was loading my gear it really hit me. I just sat in the back of my van and cried. He was the first close friend who I lost and far, far too soon."

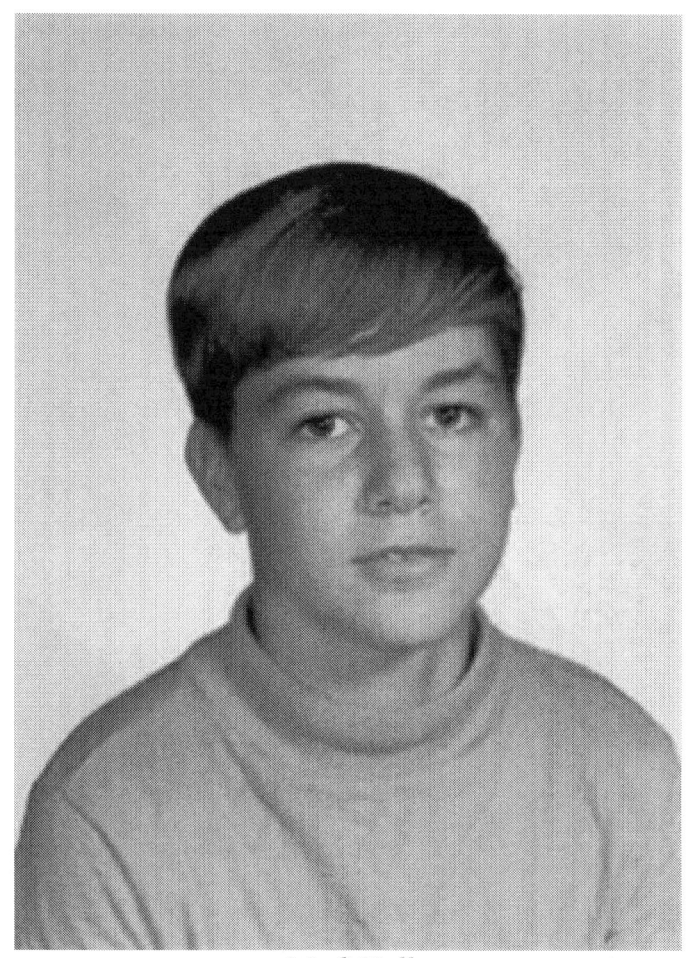

Mark Null

Remembering Edmund Ponikiewski, Greg Cober said:

"Edmund was faster than greased lightning. I remember him being on the MacArthur High School track team, and whenever there was a meet, Ed was first out of the line-up. I think he set a few school track records!"

Ed Ponikiewski

I can attest to Edmund's speed, since I once saw him in action, but not on the track. Ed Ponikiewski once won a blue ribbon for me in a swim meet competition. He was the final man on a four-man swim team; we were losing until Ed dove into the water, where he passed other swimmers to win first place for our team. He was one of the older Scouts I looked up to. I don't ever remember him acting silly, rebellious, or disrespectful. His family owned and operated a flower shop in Irving—Dahleem's Florist. I think he understood hard work and responsibility from his family's business, and I suspect he looked at the rest of us with wonder, since many of us hadn't yet faced up to those concepts. In later life he became a photographer, taking pictures of children in Irving for their school portraits. He left behind a wife and family.

Doug Reed and Bobby Borah have passed away in recent years. They were both older scouts, I liked them both, but they were known better by the higher-ranking Scouts. According to my brother David:

"Doug Reed lived next door to the Mahaffeys, so I got to see him from time to time when I was running around with Duane Tarver. And I do mean "running around," because we were too young to drive. It was hoof it or ride a bike. I wouldn't be surprised if the Reeds got into Scouts because of Ray. I seem to recall that Doug had a job at a little ice cream parlor on Belt Line and Rochelle Roads, just behind the old 7-Eleven. I remember seeing him making up soft-serve ice cream cones and wearing a paper food-service hat. Doug and his brother Mike were both good guys—Doug was big and muscular and had the complexion of a redhead, while Mike was smaller and leaner and dark-haired. They were a lot of fun to be around, but I think they might have moved away after 1970. Doug was in my high school class, but he disappeared from my yearbooks after my freshman year. Or maybe Doug was a little older than I knew, and dropped out of high school to go into the military. At any rate, I lost track of both the Reed boys after I quit Scouts, and was very sad to learn that Doug had died."

Doug was the big brother to Mike Reed—a small and scrappy Scout who liked to fight! Doug was a big tall quiet and gentle sort. They were kind of opposites in a way. Even though he was tall, I wasn't afraid of him like I was Mike. Doug had served with the military in Vietnam, something most of us missed out on.

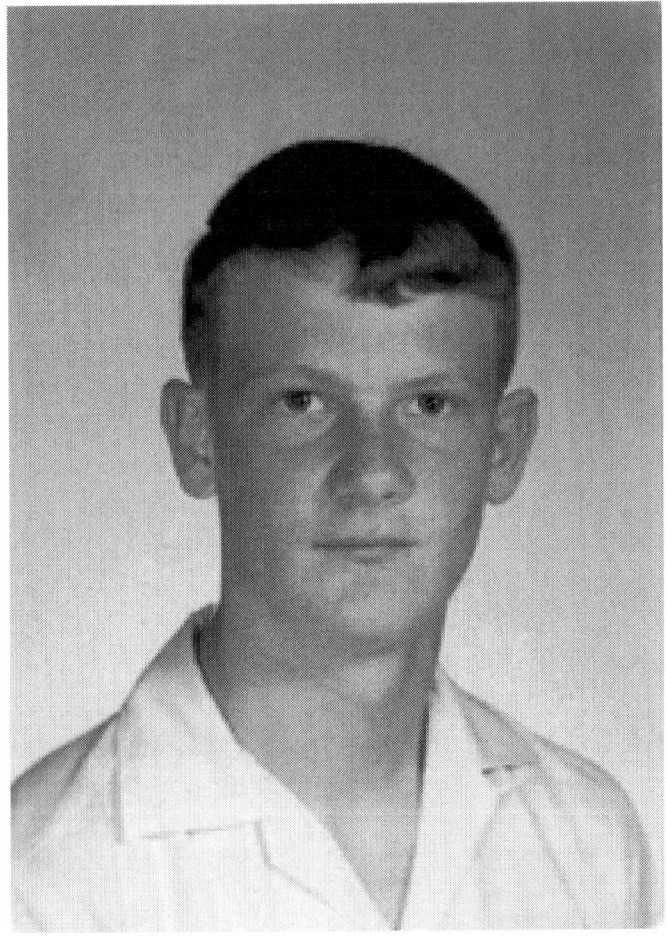

Doug Reed

Bobby Borah belonged to one of the pioneer families of Irving. They owned a farm on land that is now located in the DFW Airport area. Bobby used to work with the animals before going to school. He was quiet and mindful and was never the cause of any problems. He was the kind of Scout you could trust.

Bobby Borah

David Bennett remembers:

"Bobby was a quiet kid. I didn't get to know him very well, but recall that he was slim and wore glasses and could run real fast.

I remember seeing him run once on one of our campouts. He was wearing Boy Scout shorts with the webbed belt [and] the knee stockings we could wear when we wore shorts and moccasins. He went tearing through our campsite, and I was startled by a couple of things: (1) I could not believe how small his waist was—his legs were well-muscled, though; and (2) he had a big grin on his face, which was unusual, because he was normally very quiet. Well, split seconds after he disappeared, some other guys came tearing through my campsite, evidently chasing Bobby. Neither party stopped to talk, so I never knew exactly what had happened. It amuses me to think that Bobby may have gotten into some mischief/trouble during his Scouting days, because it seems that there may have been a spark of the devil beneath that quiet exterior."

There are other Scouts from 826 who have also passed away, but these were the ones I knew. We used to play, camp, eat, sleep, and fight with these members. We grew up together; experienced many of the same things; had common bonds, friends, and memories. Each of these Scouts has his own story. Each time I receive news that the troop has gotten smaller, it hurts.

CHAPTER TEN

BEING BRAVE AND BEING PREPARED

A Scout is Brave

This story was written by Chuck Wagner for the Troop 826 website. I include it here because it illustrates what Chuck went through to get his Camping merit badge—plus it's a good story.

NO ONE COULD TEACH us life's lessons like Mr. Street could. We were on a campout at Camp Texoma. I was 12 or 13, and I was going for my first merit badge, Camping. There were three others working on the badge that weekend, too. I remember Kevin Quine was one of them, but I'm not sure who the other two were, now.

One of the requirements for the badge was to build a shelter and sleep under it for one night. Kevin was the most naturally gifted builder/mechanic I had ever known. Even though he was only about a year older than me, he could build anything. In this case, he built the most impressive shelter I had ever seen. He found a natural indentation in one of the steep hills at Texoma. It was large enough to serve as two walls of his shelter. He planted a post and then built two walls back to the hill. Then, he built a roof over it all. He made the walls and roof by stringing binder's twine and weaving live evergreen branches throughout. We referred to it as the Hotel "Hilton." Unfortunately, Mr. Street disqualified him for using live trees in the building—an explicit no-no in the merit badge book.

My shelter was on an entirely different level. Let's just say that I have never been known for my construction skills. I found three trees, and my plan was to lash poles to them forming a triangle parallel to the ground. Then, I was going to lash some smaller poles across the triangular shape and fill it in with whatever partially leaved branches I could find lying around. Unfortunately, the trees were so far apart that I couldn't find three good poles long enough to form the triangle. My only solution was to lash a couple of poles together to span the distance between the trees. It was pretty rickety!

Mr. Street came along early in the afternoon to check on our progress. He took one look at my shelter and, needless to say, he was disappointed. He grabbed one of the sides where I had lashed two poles together and shook it. It was pretty pathetic. Finally, he took one arm and gave that side a karate chop, and the whole thing came crashing to the ground. I was devastated, but Mr. Street wasn't going to allow me to waste time whining. He didn't apologize for wrecking my shelter. Instead, he told me that he expected better from me. He let me know that I had failed, but he had faith that I could do much better.

Well, let me tell you, I was mad as all get out! But I wasn't mad at Mr. Street. I was mad at myself. I knew my shelter was terrible. I had disappointed Mr. Street, whom I revered (still do). Shame on me for trying to pass off that miserable shelter as acceptable. So I went to work on rebuilding. I worked furiously all afternoon on the same design but with a determination to make it stronger and better. Later, Mr. Street came back to inspect it, and I passed. Was that the best shelter he had ever seen? No. Truthfully, it probably wasn't much better than my first attempt. But it was a little better, a little stronger. It was serviceable, but what counted the most was that Mr. Street knew he had gotten me to give the best that I had in me. Little did I know, learning to do my best was not the only lesson in store for me this weekend.

Later that evening we all went to the campfire. I don't remember who told the story of Radiation Man that night, but before the campfire was over, Mr. Street had donned his Radiation Man gear and was stalking around the camp. His glow-in-the-dark bug eyes and chemical glow stick (we had never seen a glow stick before) down the front of his white T-shirt had us all wondering what kind of scary creature this was. Well, here was the dilemma. The Scouts who were working on Camping merit badge had to leave the safety of our fellow Scouts and the campfire and walk a mile or two to our shelters where we were required to sleep in order to pass that merit badge requirement. None of us wanted to go. Kevin, whose site was the closest to mine, decided that it didn't make sense for him to go out there and sleep since his shelter was disqualified and he was going to have to do it all over anyway. The other two Scouts were just plain scared.

So here I was, all alone, hiking through the pitch-black woods to get to my shelter. And buddy, you can believe I was some kind of scared. I bedded down, but I couldn't sleep. When you're 13 and alone in the dark woods after hearing about and seeing Radiation Man, you don't sleep. As you can imagine, I heard every sound in the woods that night, and with every sound, my flashlight was on and I was scanning the horizon for signs of Radiation Man or any other creature of the night that might be coming for me.

Why did I stay? Almost anyone who had Mr. Street as a Scoutmaster could answer that question. As I lay there that night, as scared as any Scout ever was, there was only one thing that could have been worse than falling into the clutches of Radiation Man—disappointing Mr. Street twice in one weekend. That was the kind of inspiration that Mr. Street was to me and a hundred other kids. To this day, I find myself asking, "What would Mr. Street say about what I'm doing?" By his example, he still keeps me on an even keel.

"Mr. Street had donned his Radiation Man gear and was stalking around the camp."

What did I learn? Even though I couldn't have verbalized it then, I learned that bravery is not the absence of fear. It is feeling the fear, and then going ahead and doing what you need to do, want to do, or have to do in spite of the fear. That lesson is one that has helped me so much throughout some tumultuous times since then. I learned it at 13. I learned it from Mr. Street.

I might have slept an hour or two that night. When dawn finally broke that next morning, I quickly prepared a continental breakfast, I broke camp and headed back to where the troop was camping. I rejoined my patrol where Paul Maples was putting the finishing touches on his breakfast specialty—pancakes and chili. He offered me some. I declined. After all, a Scout is brave, not stupid!

Always Be Prepared

Both Mark Dixon and Jack Rankin told me this story about how they were going fishing and frog gigging with Alvin Brown and Monte Pipes. This wasn't a Scout-sponsored activity; they had just gotten together for an outing. Jack said,

"We were frog gigging because we wanted to fry the legs, which everyone knows is good eating. We are on a farm somewhere outside of Irving. Mark Dixon proceeds to jump a fence with a frog gig in his hand. When he lands on the other side of the fence, he penetrated the gig into his thigh. The situation is bad. All the drills we had practiced for First Aid now become a reality. We thought about pulling the gig out, but the barbs had gone into the skin. . . . We got him under a shade tree and treated him for shock. Next we cut down limbs big enough to make a stretcher. We took our shirts off and manipulated them in a way where we could support Mark's weight. I carried one end of the stretcher and Monte and Alvin carried the other end. We had to go maybe two miles to a farmhouse. There was a girl there about 14 years old. She was about our age. Anyway, her parents were gone and none of us had a driver's license. That girl nonetheless drove all of us to an emergency room..."

Mark filled in some of the gaps with his version of the story:

"One time we had a bunch of the guys from the Scout troop. We all got together and decided to go over there fishing. I took a couple of spears, fishing poles, fishing tackle . . . At the end of our fun, on the way back, there was a fence that was about two feet tall. Instead of stepping over it or walking around it,

"They figured out a way to carry me with the spear still in my leg."

I hopped over it with all that stuff in my hands, and when my hands came down, the spear went right into my leg, buried it barbs and all, a three-pronged spear, about six inches above my knee. Luckily I had attached the handle with screws, so I was able to pull a screwdriver out of my tackle box and unscrew the screws. I wouldn't let anybody else touch it because it was in there scraping on the muscles down inside of my leg. The guys used their Scouting skills and built a way to carry me across about a mile of pasture, because I couldn't walk the way I was. I would have destroyed the muscles in my leg with those prongs, and I couldn't pull it out. They figured out a way to carry me with the spear still in my leg. . . . That's one of those beautiful things. If we hadn't had Scouting skills, if the guys hadn't been able to build something to get me out of there, it would have taken a heck of a lot longer and may have done a lot more damage. One of the beautiful things about Scouting, it prepares you to be prepared!"

CHAPTER ELEVEN

AWARDS

Favorite Merit Badges

I ASKED THE SCOUTS about their favorite merit badges, which probably reflected the most fun they had while on a campout or at summer camp, and Mark Dixon remembered with the following:

"I liked working on knots, but actually, I really enjoyed the Survival merit badge. I wound up teaching the survival stuff to a bunch of kids for their merit badge, tutoring them, what have you. That was always a lot of fun. I did have fun with the knots also. I remember an awesome summer camp we had where we built a tower out of timbers and wood and weren't able to use anything but ropes to put it together. That was quite a challenge and really put us to the test. That may have been the most enjoyable camp of all of them. Of course, the Canoeing merit badge was fun, too. Sinking the canoe and getting it back upright and getting back into it, that was fun."

Chuck Wagner shared his recollections with me:

"Definitely Camping, that's where some of those stories came from [and] Canoeing: I've always loved the water. In fact, I think I got the Canoeing merit badge before I got the Camping merit badge. I started the Camping, and it required so many campouts to complete it, and in between them, I got Canoeing. The Printing merit badge was another one that I enjoyed a lot, and it was influential, obviously, because that's the career path

I've taken. I remember vividly going over to Mr. Johnson's, Calvin Johnson's house, four or five of us. He taught the Printing merit badge . . . Mr. Johnson was a sign-maker by trade. He had a miter saw and any number of jigsaws and different things there at his house, and he would do a lot of that at home where he would create signs out of plastic, cut them out, put them together. Sometimes they'd be backlit.

Patches from Chuck Wagner's collection. Patch trading and collecting became one of his hobbies while in Scouts.

One of the requirements was we had to make our own printing press, and we made our own little silkscreen printing press. He got us the fabric and showed us how to tack it up, and showed us how to make stencils, and we'd make our screen, and we'd get the ink, and we'd squeegee it back and forth. We had to make 50 copies of something, silkscreen printed, so that was one of my favorite ones. There were lots of good badges."

Mike Huebner shared with me that his favorite merit badges were Rifle and Shotgun:

"I remember the details of getting the merit badge. I remember shooting .22s. You had to shoot a certain number of targets with a certain score. And then, the shotgun part was real limited, you only shot it five or six times . . . I think because it was more expensive to buy shotgun shells. You could buy .22 shells cheap; oddly enough, that's become my big hobby. I shoot rifle competition with black powder cartridge rifles."

Monte Pipes' favorite was Cycling. He recalled a Scouting memory, saying:

"Mike Quine, Ray Mahaffey, and I rode our bikes from Irving to Keller on the back roads primarily through where the DFW Airport is now. We stayed overnight at my Grandmother's in Keller and rode back the next day. We had to have two trips of 25 miles, and this outing covered both. It was pretty cool to have that freedom as a young guy."

In my own case, the one merit badge that was the most memorable, but not exactly the most fun, was Hiking. We had to learn a lot about foot care, blisters, bandages, cramps, heat exhaustion, and safety. This was definitely a badge we earned. My mother would drive a carload of us 10 miles away from home and drop us off; it was up to us to walk back. In the summer, we'd leave early in the a.m., hoping to make it home by noon before the heat became too unbearable. I was fifteen, an older scout then, but I still found ways to get blistered. By the time we had to make the 20-mile hike, we knew what to expect and had toughened-up to it. We took no chances, carrying canteens, pocket change (for cokes at any 7-Eleven we found on our way back), hats, sunglasses, and loose clothes. We looked like walking tourists.

The Court of Honor

The Court of Honor was held every few months, perhaps twice a year or once a quarter, to recognize the boys who had made some progress toward earning merit badges and receiving their next rank. This was always a special time for the boys and their families, since parents were also invited. Many times food would be served—lots of good eating in a picnic-style spread. After eating, the troop meeting was held and skits, one for each patrol, were performed so that there would be at least four or five skits, enough so there would be a few laughs. After some singing, the serious business of dispersing the medals began.

Since the regular Scout didn't know what was involved in a Court of Honor ceremony, it was up to the troop leadership to guide the festivities. The lights were dimmed, candles were lit; and once they were, a hush fell over the crowd. Parents, sitting in the back rows, were quiet during this time, and everyone waited. The boys whose names were called would come to the front. Their parents would accompany them many times to share in the honor. Rank was pinned on the Scouts' uniforms, and pictures were taken. This was almost a reverent time, a moment of awe, probably the most special time of the year for the Scout. Mr. Street would speak about the things that were involved in achieving the merit badge or rank; and for a moment, that boy would feel like a deserving member of the Boy Scouts. This was his moment in front of the troop and the other scouts' families, something he wouldn't forget as long as he lived. He may not have achieved honor in school or at church, but here for a few moments with the Boy Scouts, he felt his worth.

Kevin Quine at the Court of Honor, with his father, Hilton Quine. Ray Mahaffey Jr. is in the background, and it's Christmastime, 1969, at the Scout Hut. This is my favorite Scout picture.

The Totin' Chip
Originally written for the Troop 826 website in 2006.

In the world of Scouting, the ability to carry and use a hatchet or a knife was a privilege to be earned through attendance at a class on sharp instrument safety, which also included the saw and the long-handled axe. Since survival on campouts depended on a Scout's ability to use and demonstrate safety with these cutting instruments, it was one of the first classes taught to new Scouts.

If a Scout collects firewood or cuts ropes or even whittles a neckerchief slide, then he must pass this class on safety. Usually it just entailed an actual demonstration of safety techniques from Mr. Street or one of the older Scouts, or maybe a summer camp demonstration, where many outdoor classes were formally offered.

After attending this outdoor class, Mr. Street would give us our wallet-sized certificate of proof for attending this safety class. I learned some good theories here, and to this day I never carry a knife or sharp instrument without thinking how I might fall on it, so I carry it away from me, with the sharp end pointing in any direction except toward me.

We were supposed to have this document on us whenever we were cutting firewood, which would be proof to the adult supervision that we knew what we were doing.

Mr. Street made it clear to us that if he saw us violating safety practices, he would ask for our document (our "totin' chip") and then tear a corner off of it. If or when a Scout had all four corners torn off, Mr. Street would then tear the document in two, and the disgraced Scout would then have to take this safety class all over again. No older Scout wanted to do that, since he would be thrown back into a class with younger Scouts. This would represent a loss of face for him. It was unthinkable.

I remember also receiving a wooden totin' chip, about an inch in diameter and 1/3 inch in width, sanded, with the words 'Totin' Chip' written across the surface with a black felt-tipped pen (or magic marker). This was a nice memento to have. I kept it for the longest time. It signified trust.

Well, life went on.

I was with the Eagle Patrol on a campout, sitting around the tent one day, doing nothing special. Different patrols used to camp far away from each other, and on this trip, we were in a wooded area. I was with my brother David, the leader of Eagle Patrol at that time. We had a lull in activity. We had been cooking, but now had all the equipment clean, and were waiting for the next activity to begin. We never knew what to expect.

One of the Scouts began to throw his knife in a manner that we all knew was unsafe, but since he was older we weren't going to say anything. He was actually pretty good! He would throw it at a tree, and it would stick. This impressed us younger Scouts. David was watching also, and being bored, thought he'd try his hand at it. So sitting on his folding chair he spotted the nearest tree, took aim, and let the knife fly.

The knife went to the tree, bounced off the bark and back toward the ground, bounced off the ground and back into David's knee. The knife's path had made a perfect triangle.

David fell over backward in pain, but kept himself from yelling out loud. The knife didn't stick in him, just created a deep clean puncture wound. Two other Scouts were there and jumped to his aid; Richard Dahlgren was one. I think he had been throwing the knife in the beginning, so he may have felt responsible.

Good thing these Scouts had also taken a first-aid class.

Soon, another troop activity would be starting. It might be a hike or a swim, so we began covering up this great crime of carelessness.

The Eagle Patrol cleaned and bandaged David's knee in double time talking only in hushed whispers. If anyone asked David about the bandage, he could just say that he had tripped or fallen, something manly, and not mention stabbing himself in the knee. The physical pain had stopped, but was replaced with the pain of fear—fear that Mr. Street might find out. There was an understanding among the Scouts not to say anything

about this since our Patrol Leader (and a few others) might lose totin' chip privileges, and be forced to take the safety class over again with younger Scouts. This would be unbearable. We were all one.

Here was a demonstration for me of how easy it was to hurt yourself unintentionally. Safety became a real concept that day; it wasn't just a theory anymore.

David said I could tell this story, now.

David Bennett, 6th Grade, A.S. Johnston Elementary, 1966-67. Member of the Eagle Patrol.

CHAPTER TWELVE

HONOR AND FORGIVENESS
AND LOVE

Scout's Honor

AT MY FIRST CAMPING EXPERIENCE at Camp Wisdom, I was kicked out of a cooking class for referring to one of the staff members as 'Crow Nose.' He had a big nose. I guess I didn't need to point it out. He was also a nice guy, and I should have kept my observations to myself. Well, this got back to the troop, and it caused a minor scandal when it reached the adult supervision at our campsite. Someone tattled. I was told on by one of my fellow Troop members, but I don't know who did it. If I found out, there might have been retribution, so ignorance was a good thing. Mr. Mahaffey was one of the adult volunteers at the camp at that time. He was the only adult present, and I had to explain to him how I got myself kicked out of that particular cooking class. Mr. Mahaffey was one of the more stable, quiet, and consistent volunteers that Troop 826 had. He was also the Committee Chairman for the Troop. That means he was the point of contact when it came to gathering equipment for the troop, making purchases, raising money, being a parent liaison, and so on. A lot of different responsibilities came with being the Committee Chairman, which was a "catch-all" title.

So there I was, at age 11, on my first camping experience, having to give an account of myself to the Troop Committee Chairman. Why I referred to this unknown camp staff member as 'Crow Nose' I don't know, since as I mentioned previously, he was a nice person, an older Scout. I think I was tired and didn't want to have to clean up after the cooking was done. It seemed to me that there was always one more job to do before the task was finished.

Mr. Mahaffey listened to my story, then he said he wanted me to do something, something he trusted me to do. He wanted me to go back to the camp staffer and apologize for my outburst. He said he wasn't going to follow-up on me to see if I did the apologizing or not. I was completely on my honor. Maybe then I could get back into the cooking class and learn how to feed myself on future campouts, and maybe even earn a Cooking merit badge.

Well, I saw my out here. I told him I would and left the camp-site, heading toward the cooking area as though I were going to apologize.

But that's not what I did. Instead I played Boy Scout hooky and went exploring Camp Wisdom, hiking the trails, seeing the sites, enjoying nature until it was time for swimming.

Other Scout members wanted to know if I got in trouble or not, and I told them "no." I had got away with it. I had beaten the system. Not having any idea what honor was all about, I relied on my cleverness.

There was only one drawback to this; that being, I had lied to a good man, a man who was there to help all of us Scouts. I supposed he thought everyone was as honest as he was. It might not have occurred to him that there were people like me who would look for a way out through any means possible. But that's what I did. If Mr. Mahaffey were a *bad* man, it wouldn't have bothered me a bit to lie to him; however, I knew him to be a good man, and I had taken advantage of the situation. I figured I had enough authority in my life, what with family, church, and school. I didn't need or want a camp staff member or anybody else telling me what to do.

It's been over 40 years, and this still bothers me; I didn't count on having a conscience. I never did tell Mr. Mahaffey that I didn't go apologize to the camp staffer. If confession is good for the soul, I'm putting it here as a written confession. Mr. Mahaffey may not even remember the situation. He put the responsibility in my lap and probably forgot all about it.

I have sinned and done wrong. I lied to a good man. I took the easy way out. I didn't live up to any kind of Scouting ideals that I had at the time, and I didn't learn how to clean up after cooking. And what about the insulted camp staffer? I wasn't aware of his name; I've never seen him since. But you know, he really did have a big nose.

A Bump in the Night

At our Thursday-night troop meetings, Mr. Street would usually give us a half hour of recreation so we could burn off any extra energy we had, which meant the last half hour of the troop meeting would go fairly smoothly.

Once outside the Scout Hut, we Scouts had already decided to play British Bulldog, a game guaranteed to take any remaining energy out of us.

To play, all the Scouts line up behind a boundary on the far side of the backyard field. Only a few of the larger and older Scouts are free to roam about in the middle. These few Scouts then yell "British bulldog," and all the Scouts on the far side of the field run through the middle to the other safe, far side, marked boundary. During this run they try to avoid being caught by the older, larger Scouts. Those unfortunate enough to be captured struggle to be free, but if the older Scouts manage to hold and lift them up off the ground long enough to yell "1-2- 3 British bulldog," the captured Scout immediately becomes part of the middle team. He will now assist in the capture of the remaining running Scouts.

After watching all the struggling, the Scouts in the safe boundary would be rested enough for another round; the Scouts in the middle would again yell "British bulldog." This goes on until all the Scouts are captured. With only one or two runners left, they would eventually be caught, captured, and lifted up. I suppose they could be considered the winners, but since they become part of the other team in the end, in reality they were only the last survivors. It was a game we all loved to play; it was a feat of skill, speed, and strength.

One winter's dark night, we went out to the back of the Scout Hut to play this game. I was among the runners, doing fairly well, considering my age (12). The middle team was getting large, and they yelled "British bulldog" to get us to run again. I took off ahead of the rest of my team, because I didn't want to be in the middle of a running pack, where you were slowed down, making you an easier target to be picked off. The only light we had that night was the back porch light, which was fairly bright and lit up the whole back field.

I could see Mike Huebner on the other team in the middle, but didn't figure he'd be any problem since he was shorter and lighter than me. There was no way he could hold me for the others to lift me up. I did see Mike starting to get in my way, but by that time I had built up speed and would soon be too fast to catch. I figured Mike would try to tackle me anyway, but then he just disappeared, and tripped me! I went down, angry with myself for letting Mike trick me. I figured I'd have to get up quickly before any others on the middle team could pounce on me.

I sat up just in time to see the knee of the fattest Scout in the troop, who also happened to be one of the runners, just before it made contact with my forehead above my right eye. The fat

Scout fell over me and began nursing his knee. I saw stars and fell back to the ground, screaming like a stuck pig. The game stopped for a moment, long enough to move both of us off the playing field. Then they resumed playing.

Well, I tried to play some more, but couldn't work up the energy. The game soon ended, and we were all back in the Scout Hut, carrying on with our Scout duties, only I couldn't concentrate on what was being said. I sat in my pew and moaned and groaned. The knee to my head was somehow affecting the rest of me. The room was moving, so I got up and walked to the back, telling Mr. Street that I was sick. I think Mr. Street was concerned about me, but he had to watch the rest of the troop, and another Scout leader offered to give me a ride home.

I think this man's name was Mr. Weaver, the stepfather of Rod Egger, member of the Eagle Patrol. I don't remember much about the trip home, except feeling better after I threw up on the cab floor, then feeling bad about having messed up his truck.

He got me home, and I went straight to the couch. Mr. Weaver told Mom that I managed to bump my head. I let him tell it because injuries sound more formal, more serious when coming from adults. I got to spend the next day at home lying in bed, missing school, and making a miraculous recovery in time for the weekend, which I would waste on television and looking for ways to be entertained, as kids with no job or goals do.

Thirty years came and went, and one day I met up with Mike Huebner while walking my postal route. We got reacquainted and have been in touch since. One day Mike said, "You know, I've always felt bad about one thing, and that's the day I tripped you when we were playing British Bulldog. You got hurt because of me, and I'm sorry about that."

Well, I never faulted Michael for my getting hurt! How long had he carried that guilt around with him? Over 30 years? That's a long time to be carrying an unnecessary misunderstanding or burden around.

But I knew immediately what he was talking about, since that episode had been driven into my skull by a charging rhinoceros-Scout, and I said, "Mike, you did exactly what I would have done. I've never been mad at you. I was only mad at myself for letting myself get tripped up! And don't worry about my getting hurt, because I milked that and managed to miss a day of school, which I didn't care for."

This gave Mike some needed guilt relief. Now he knew for certain I'd never harbored any blame for him and was sure that there was no brain damage done to me. Pretty sure, anyhow. I had gone back to the Scout Hut the next week for the troop meeting. Nothing was said about my head bump. The swelling had mostly gone down by then anyway. No lawsuits were filed; no hospitalization or legal action threatened. We took our lumps and that's how we liked it. We were Scouts, learning how to be men. We had fun.

An early shot of Troop 826 with Mr. Street on the far right.

A Token

There's one piece of the Boy Scout uniform that allowed for individuality, and that was the piece right under the chin of any Boy Scout: the neckerchief slide. For some Scouts, a piece of wood, a cross-section of a small tree or branch would do. This could be dried, sanded, varnished, painted, shaped, whatever the Scout's imagination would allow. Of course he mustn't forget to nail, staple, or glue a strap to the back of the wood to allow the neckerchief to slide through. Many variations of this can be seen in Boy Scout camping and summer camp photos. This little piece of wood signified a Scout's closeness to nature.

The neckerchief slide I chose was found at home, not in the wild. At our house, we grew up with Friday-night horror shows on television, so we were exposed to Frankenstein, Dracula, the Mummy, and then later, sci-fi monsters. It followed that, whenever allowed, we brought home plastic model figures of these Hollywood horror figures. One of the figures that made it into our home was King Kong.

King Kong was a giant gorilla that really meant no harm. He was just a big dumb ape looking for love. We kept him in our bedroom, along with the other monster figures, and over the years these plastic statuettes would meet with abuse, wear, tear, and disrepair. Some of these figures lasted longer than others. King Kong was made of sturdy stuff. He outlasted all the rest, until one day, he too fell apart.

Instead of throwing him away, I looked at the pieces to see what could be salvaged. The gorilla's face had fallen away from the rest of his body. I looked at it; it looked at me. It would live again as a neckerchief slide.

I managed to wait until there was only a small amount of time left, then I asked Daddy if he'd make a slide out of the plastic face for me. He wondered what it was for, and I told him. Of course this was just a few hours from the weekly Scout meeting on Thursday night, so Daddy had to move fast. All the tools were in the garage, and I knew he'd figure something out. I'd communicated my part, the want; the rest was up to him.

He took this plastic face and figured out what would make a good back piece to it. Since he worked with electronics, he had different sized wires lying about. He drilled a hole in each of King Kong's temples and pushed a thick copper wire through them, cutting them off on the outside and bending them toward the back, something I couldn't do since I'm sure I would have broken the plastic with my youthful impatience.

This slide was great. Nobody else had one like it. When you looked at the Scout, you'd see the ape just below his chin. David who had a far steadier hand for detail work than I did painted it originally. This slide lasted for years. Thanks, Daddy. I took it and ran. I got lots of favorable comments on the slide by my fellow Scouts and Scout leaders.

In the years since that slide was made, it spent much time in desks, closet space, boxes, wherever you store things you just can't bring yourself to part with. Sometime after college I came home and decided that space was more important than my childhood toys, room had to be made for modern living, and so out it went with other memorabilia.

Years have come and gone since then, and I find myself wishing I had that little neckerchief slide again. It didn't take up much space. I could have worn it at scouting reunions! It's just a little something that I miss, kind of like the totin' chip. It was an original slide, one that you didn't see very often, something that had a second life, something painted by my brother and then fashioned by my father, and worn by me. Daddy wouldn't remember it if I were to remind him of it, but it was something he made for me under a time constraint (due to my lack of planning), just a little something that showed he loved me.

1. 1960's Aurora King Kong. 2. Face of Kong, which became separated from the model. 3. Drilled holes and used thick copper wire for homemade slide. 4. Happy camper, the envy of other Scouts, with his coveted neckerchief slide.

CHAPTER THIRTEEN

SCOUTS GONE BAD

Cheap Vice

I COULD NEVER FIGURE OUT what the allure, the draw, of grapevine was to young Scouts on the campout. Whenever we camped near a lake or a body of water, somehow we managed to find grapevine. We all knew that grapevine was obtainable while camping, and since we didn't have access to cigarettes (or money), this would be the cheap and easy way to explore one of the pleasures of adulthood forbidden to us: smoking!

One of the older Scouts found a dried vine, and using his Scout knife, cut it to a size acceptable for smoking. He lit it with his campfire matches, smoked it for a while, then offered it to me. I took a puff, but not finding any pleasure (or taste) in it, gave it back. He was content with his grapevine. He was committing a violation and knew it. If we were caught by the adults, we'd be in trouble. We didn't know what kind of trouble, so we tried not to think about it.

I've heard different versions of the following, but the way I remember it was, Mr. Street once caught two boys chewing tobacco on a campout. They were Alvin Brown and Monte Pipes. He knew what they were up to. Since they were out and away from the rest of the camp, they must have been up to no good. Mr. Street could hear them talking and sneaked up from behind, then pounced with his booming voice: "What are you two boys doing? Are you chewing tobacco?!"

Troop 826, circa 1971. Mr. Street can be seen in the middle with the smaller Scouts. Red berets were a part of the uniform at that time.

Alvin Brown admitted his crime, but Monte Pipes had swallowed any evidence against him.

Monte wasn't very productive for the remainder of that campout. I understand he lay sick in his tent that night and most of Saturday. I'm not sure if he ever admitted to enjoying the forbidden product.

Rehabilitation

As Scoutmaster, and on campouts, Mr. Street had a way of settling arguments, deciding cases, or meting out punishment. It was all fair, quick, and simple. He was the judge and jury. The Scouts of 826 understood that. What he said was *law.*

It's not that there was any real *fear* of Mr. Street. We all knew he liked fun just as much as the troop members did. It's just that someone had to call the shots, make the rules, and set the boundaries. Mr. Street did not shirk his responsibility here.

An episode that illustrates this Scout Law system well was the case of the cursing Scout. There was one particular Boy Scout who, on frequent occasions, would curse. He was well versed at it. It came natural to many of the Scouts, but most knew it wouldn't go well if you were to curse within earshot of Mr. Street. This one Scout made that mistake on a campout. He dropped the "F-bomb" too close to Mr. Street, and there was no question about whether the Scoutmaster had heard him.

Mr. Street knew he was dealing with a habitual curser. This boy's character was in need of repair. Since the swearing had occurred in front of the troop, the troop would be involved in the punishment. He told the boys to form the "belt line."

I asked Mr. Street about this belt line. Were there any belts involved? No, this was just hands-on punishment.

All the troop members were to gather and stand in a line, one boy behind the next, and facing in the same direction. Mr. Street would have the boys spread apart, probably four or five feet between each Scout. The Scouts were told to put their feet as far apart as they could, still standing. The offender was told his fate: His job was to crawl as fast as he could through the maze, under the line of Scouts. The Scouts would then spank the curser as he crawled under and past. If he crawled quickly, his punishment would soon be over, but if he hesitated, the more spanks he would receive.

The offending Scout was not happy with his fate. The idea was greater than he could bear, and he protested with "I'm going to tell my mama!" to which Mr. Street said, "Go ahead!"

Well, the Scout's last bluff didn't work, so he started crawling. Mr. Street was in the line also. He said he probably shouldn't have been, but he was. The older Scouts were good spankers. The younger ones weren't as strong, but they could be creative if they were quick enough to find cow patties to place in the crawling path. That would give the offender something else to avoid if he were able.

The punishment was swift. The curser took his medicine like a trooper. He was now cured. There was never any report of him running home to tell his mama, something all *real* boys just don't do (especially if they're guilty). This episode was over, except for the comedy of it all. You have to wonder if any Scout could mete out, or even receive, such a clear brand of justice in today's world.

CHAPTER FOURTEEN

INDIAN GEORGE

IRVING RESIDENT GEORGE ALFORD was known by all Scouts and children in the Dallas area as "Indian George." That's what he called himself around them, and he wanted us to call him that as well. That's how we'd remember him!

Mr. Alford was born December 29, 1914; a full-blooded Comanche. He grew up in east Oklahoma, and in his youth he became a Junior Forest Ranger before entering the service for World War II. Wounded during the war and awarded the Purple Heart, he made his way back to the United States by troop ship, and observed, after the ship had docked, some boys offering help to the arriving soldiers by carrying their duffle bags and personal equipment. As Mr. Street said, "George wanted to know who those helpful boys were." They were Boy Scouts, and at that moment, Mr. Alford thought he'd like to become involved with a group of young men like those. That was the beginning of Mr. Alford's affiliation with the Boy Scouts.

While in Dallas, Mr. Alford helped establish Troop and Post 134 for which he served as Scoutmaster for a time. After moving to Irving in 1964, Mr. Alford, still active with the Scouting programs, visited the local schools and shared his knowledge of Indian lore with the schoolchildren, most whom had never seen a Native American close up, especially not one who knew so much about his people and who could share his knowledge in an entertaining way.

*George Alford portrait displayed at BSA Camp Wisdom, Dallas,
Texas. The artist is Barbara Turrentine-Fryrear*

In a tape-recorded interview Mr. Alford told of his school
visitations.[1] He had inherited many Native American artifacts
from his grandfather and kept suitcases filled with them to take

to the schools. He wished for the children to hold them, to handle and experience them. He'd take his drum to the high schools, and when he wished for silence, he would beat the drum four times, and afterward you could hear a pin drop—the principal wished he had something that worked as well. The teachers noticed there were too many people gathering around him in the classroom, so they moved him to the auditorium where all the students could hear and see him.

He showed a great deal of patience with children. One story from his taped interview tells how some children managed to break one of his artifacts, upsetting the children to the point of crying. Mr. Alford didn't get mad; in fact, he made a joke of it, much to the children's relief. To him it wasn't his items that were important, but rather, the children.

He said that there used to be a large Comanche settlement where the University of Dallas is now, with another where the Irving City Hall was located (now the offices of the Irving fire station). Shady Grove and Irving Boulevard served as cattle trails back when the cattle were driven to Fort Worth, the major cattle center of North Texas. Often, American Indians would expect or demand a few head of cattle when they passed through the area. When these requests were denied, the Indians would wait until nightfall before "borrowing" a few, in George's words. He had fun in his talks about the local American Indians. He said in one article that whenever they won a fight, there'd been a massacre, but when the white man won, it was known as a "battle."

In 1965, he started his first Indian dance team, which became bigger and better for several years, peaking with his "Santank Dance Team" in 1970.[2]

He had dug up arrowheads from the original Texas Stadium site (in Irving), when the area was being bulldozed in 1968–69. He found a pail of them himself, and remarked that if a person

147

were to follow the Trinity River, he would find more evidence of Comanches, since no Comanche would set up a teepee unless water was nearby. He donated many of his found items to the Smithsonian.

He was a fixture with local Scouts; all of the Irving troops knew him. He and Mr. Street were friends, and he would come out to the Scout Hut for Troop 826 on visits. We Scouts knew we were in for a treat when he visited, because he'd bring along his equipment and headgear and play his drum while we'd run along outside in attempts to earn a merit badge. It was a magical time, watching and listening to him on the drum, singing along while we ran. He wasn't one of our troop leaders specifically. He was a friend and leader to all the troops in Irving. It was almost like a blessing when he'd come to visit. As Eagle Scout Mike Quine put it, "All the kids loved him."

My mother Marjorie Bennett would attend parent/teacher meetings, and also Cub Scout and Boy Scout parental meetings. She told me that George Alford had attended one of those meetings and spoke on the subject of Scouting. He was very involved with the youth, even to the point of visiting Scout groups at homes. He told the mothers, "When I help your sons on their projects, I don't want or need any money for the labor; however, if you'd make me a sandwich, that's something I would not refuse." I believe Mr. George was a well-fed counselor.

Kevin Kendro, Archivist at the Irving Library, told me that his parents' backyard fence was shared by Mr. Alford's backyard. Mr. Kendro remembered how there were always young people visiting Mr. Alford, working on their merit badges, and he remembered hearing the drum beating from across the yards. We both agreed it was a good thing, since any learning activity might be helping the kids in the neighborhood from getting into any trouble. Mr. Alford helped the kids learn something and earn their Indian Lore merit badge, keeping them occupied and productive. These were traits that would help anyone later on in life.

One memory I have of Mr. Alford was after I had left Scouting and had graduated from high school. I was driving around with a school friend, Buddy Skipper, who had a paper route after college hours. We were visiting people so he could make his collections for the paper, and we came to 150 North St. Claire. Buddy had been talking about this neat Indian man who would tell him stories, but I wasn't really tuned in to what he'd been saying. I was expecting to see a man from Nepal or Bombay. Instead, the door opened to a face that was somehow familiar to me. I blurted out, "Hey! You're Indian George!" His face brightened, and he laughed and invited us in, so we entered and sat attentively while he told us stories of old Irving, and about the Native Americans who settled this area.

While cleaning up a photograph of him obtained from the *Irving Daily News*,[3] I was speaking about it to my little brother Stephen, who had been a member of another troop, Troop 821. He said he remembered Mr. Alford from one of the good deeds the Scouts of his troop used to do, which was to go over to his house and take care of the yard, also earning some kind of merit for this.

If there was any fault with Mr. Alford, it may have been that he was too easy when it came to giving credit for a Scout's achievements. This may have something to do with Mr. Alford's popularity among the local Scouts, but there was more to it than that.

He was a recognized figure among all the young as an authentic and knowledgeable American Indian. I heard one college professor say that it's in a student's favor to have at least one easy class while they're trying to get a degree, which easily translates to Scouting. Anybody can discourage a Scout,

but it takes encouragement to keep a Scout going. I'm not saying a merit badge should be a 'given,'
 but sometimes it helps when you know an adult is in your corner.

I understand that Mr. Alford would make space in his home for young men who had no home of their own to go to and have heard that he housed as many as 20 in need of help through the years.

He attended many Eagle ceremonies and was a fixture and prominent speaker there. It was an honor to have Mr. Alford preside over your Eagle ceremony as he did for the boys of Troop 826.

According to Mr. Alford's obituary,[4] he was a member of Saint Luke's Catholic Church, a member of the Disabled American Veterans (Post # 31), American Legion (Posts # 356 and 218), the Senior Citizens Band, and the Irving YMCA. He had been given the Silver Beaver Award by the Boy Scouts and was Scoutmaster Emeritus of Troops 134 and 508. He was an honorary member of the Girl Scouts and Campfire Girls and a lifetime member of the PTA. He was 69 when he died on August 7, 1984.

---

[1] Audiotape interview with George Alford conducted by Estelle Bates and Mildred Eigenbrot, probably from the mid-1970s. Printed transcript supplied by Irving Public library Archivists Jan Hart and Kevin Kendro.

[2] www.troop508irving.org/history (Scout Troop 508's website).

[3] *Irving Daily News*, October 10, 1967, page 1.

[4] *Irving Daily News,* August 8, 1984, obituary column.

*Mr. Alford was an honored guest at many Eagle ceremonies in
North Texas. Eagle Scout Steve Rackley and Mr. Alford, 1978.*

CHAPTER FIFTEEN

A SCOUT IS REVERENT

The Prayer Circle

A T THE CLOSE OF OUR WEEKLY MEETINGS at the Scout Hut, the troop would sometimes hold a prayer. We all got up out of our seats and formed a circle. The lights would dim to darkness, and we were told to bow our heads and go down the line praying. One Scout was to say something like "Thank you, Lord, for the good weather." Another Scout would say, "Please take care of the sick and elderly." Another might say, "Thank you for our good health."

The prayer was getting closer to me, a new Scout. I was 11 years old, and I certainly didn't like speaking in front of people, not unless I had something memorized or was reading from a page. I didn't know how to lead a prayer. I didn't know what's important or relevant to the troop. All I knew was what I saw on the evening news each night, and since this was in the 1960s, war, riots, and college unrest were the big stories. I didn't understand the Vietnam War, didn't know what the riots were about, but I did know what a teenager was.

So here comes the prayer. It was my turn to say something. I say "Lord, please do something about all those bad teenagers." That's it. I did my part. The prayer got passed on down the line, to my relief.

Prayer is a solemn thing. We're talking to God here, concentrating on things above. So why is it I hear Ray Mahaffey Jr., an older Scout, begin to stifle a laugh?

Jack Rankin is next to him. He's trying to keep from giggling. Across the circle someone tries to keep quiet. The next Scout is praying, but he's having a hard time getting the words out.

I'd laugh too, but I don't know what the joke is all about. There are about four Scouts now who are trying to keep from laughing. Good thing it's dark and we couldn't see each other's faces or else there might be more giggling.

After a minute or two of this, before the prayer got to the end of the circle, the "Amen" part, Mr. Street booms, "All right! That's enough of that!" then he throws on the lights, saying, "That's it. Go home. Meeting's over, see you next week! That's *no way* to have a prayer!"

Some of the Scouts could now laugh out loud. Others said, "Attaboy Bennett!" "Way to go!" What did I do?

Somehow, I'd unintentionally busted up a prayer meeting. Things like this certainly didn't encourage a Scout toward public speaking.

The Chapel Service

At the Reunion Campout in 2006, we boys (now grown men) gathered for the Sunday morning chapel service after breakfast. No one even had to tell us, guide us, or order us to attend; this time we wanted to be there!

The Reunion was winding down, and we were almost ready to leave. Who knows when we'd have another gettogether? Each Scout was given time to say whatever it was he wanted to the small group. Jerry Thetford stood up and said how he really wasn't sure what this campout would do for him, but it turned out that it meant more to him than he counted on, being here for the weekend, catching up with his friends and Mr. Street. Mike Quine did the same and would later take photos of us as a group. I'm not much of a public speaker, so I had to think quick; my time was coming up.

The 826 Reunion Campout at the Chapel Gathering
Front row: Jerry Thetford, Mr. Street, Steve Safran, Chuck Wager.
Back row: Steve Rackley, Mike Quine, Richard Bennett.
Alan Walls is not seen.

When I did talk, I spoke of a conversation that I once had with Mr. Street, apologizing to him for not going all the way to Eagle. I said that his reply to me was that Scouting was not an Eagle factory, meaning that we were there for the fellowship and friendship as boys. Most of us wouldn't go all the way with it. Scouting meant much more than ranks, it was our time together. We wouldn't forget our almost kindred-like bond. I said I wished my brother David had been there with us. Then I glanced over at Mike Quine and said, "I wish Kevin (his deceased brother) were here as well. Everyone here knew and loved Kevin Quine," and all were nodding "Yes," "That's right." I think I said something right that day, for a change.

Mr. Street spoke last. He said, "I want to thank God for allowing me the privilege of being here again with you boys. You don't know what this does for me to see you all grown and carrying the responsibilities that you do. I hope we'll be able to have more Reunions. At my age, I know there aren't many years left for me. I just want to thank you for being here and . . . I love you." And with that we all said almost in unison, "And we love you too, Mr. Street!"

CHAPTER SIXTEEN

LOOKING TOWARD THE FUTURE

THINKING ON MY DAYS with the Boy Scouts and Troop 826 gives me a sense of gratitude for Mr. Street and the volunteers who helped make our time with Scouting worth remembering. For me, though, these experiences remain in the past. For any young Scout reading this, your experiences are in the future. If you want, you can go far, perhaps even to Eagle. I've already pointed out that it's my belief that any Scout who makes it that far has, for the most part, learned much of what he needs to know to be successful in his adult life. If you are willing, go as far as you can in your youth.

On the pages that follow are suggestions and recommendations that should help in your attaining that goal. Learn from the mistakes and successes of yourself and others:

1. You cannot do this on your own. You'll need help. If you ever want to do something beyond yourself, you should look around to see who could help you:

a. Make friends in the troop who share your goals . . . to go as far as you can in your Scouting career.

b. Work with these friends to accomplish your goals and merit badges.

c. Seek adult supervision . . . ask "Can you help me?" and never "Will you do this for me?" Any good and capable adult will be glad to help a young person who has goals, who is trying to accomplish something worthwhile. To adults, a young person with goals is a rare find.

Future Eagle Scouts Mike Quine, Ray Mahaffey Jr., and Jack Rankin – friends with a common goal.

2. Avoid getting bogged down in other activities that will take you away from your goals. As Chuck Wagner said, he was too busy with other worthy endeavors to concentrate on his own Scouting career. He enjoyed his Order of the Arrow activities. He helped many others with it, but it cost him his main goal, the Eagle Badge.

3. You'll need information when learning about a new subject. When looking for information, Wikipedia is a good starting point (in your personal computer). Presently, it can give you an introduction to most merit badge subjects. You'll eventually need to dig deeper, and for this, the public library is your best friend. You can check out books and read until you're fully knowledgeable on any subject. If you're going to share or teach others, you'll need to know what you're talking about.

4. Help others. Personally, I couldn't stand the idea of being a leader. That meant responsibility, which at the time was too much for me to willingly accept. If you are like I was, then make up your mind that you will be a good follower. A leader is really just someone who influences others . . . and you can do the same in the follower capacity. As a follower, you're actually more free to work on your merit badges. Neither is better, since all people are different. Both types can be a help to fellow troop members.

5. Take things a small piece at a time. My brother (David) said he was daunted by the task of 21 merit badges. He said if he had broken it all down into small, manageable pieces, he wouldn't have been afraid of it. If you do the same, you'll eventually be able to accomplish much, with patience.

6. Summer camp is a great place to get many of your basic merit badges out of the way. Here's the story of what happened with me at a summer camp when I was around 12 or 13 years old. On about the 4th day of this camp, I was walking down a trail with a couple of scouts, when Mr. Hart, a troop volunteer/dad stopped us. Mr. Hart liked working with kids having done the same thing as a little league coach and Cub Scout Pack Leader. He looked at us and said, "What are you working on?" I remember thinking, "What's he talking about?" We gave some answer like "I dunno. What are we supposed to be working on?" I actually had a blank, surprised look on my face. I didn't grasp what he was trying to say. He then went into his lecture, "What are you doing here? Don't you know you should be working on your merit badges or next rank?" After a few minutes, he walked off, disgusted by us. Well, we then went back to what we were doing, which was hiking, swimming, hanging around with others, going to the snack bar, eating the cafeteria food, participating in the Scouting songs, skits, friendships . . . and having fun! This was part of our summer vacation, after all . . . and we had other plans, which were to do as much of nothing as we could. I suppose we had too much freedom at that time, and I even resented the fact that an adult would question what I thought was part of my vacation. I had wasted a lot of my opportune time, something I also did during my public school years. Mr. Hart was trying to help us, but somehow it just didn't sink in; that meant more responsibility.

7. Write it down. I've heard it said, "If it's not on paper, it didn't happen." Again, David had mentioned to me that he would do many Scouting activities toward a goal but would forget or neglect to write it down. I was the same way. I just enjoyed being a part of the crowd, being around other Scouts. Put it on paper and put the paper in a folder. In fact, you should keep a notebook for each merit badge you're working toward. With this you can prove dates, times, activities, places, the people you were with; all of those prove that you did indeed accomplish what you set out to do. Have adults or your sponsor sign it in order to verify to anyone out there who wishes to know about your activities. By the time you finish your merit badge requirements, you will be knowledgeable on that subject, more so than the average person. Do this 21 times, and you'll be an Eagle Scout.

8. Make it fun. It doesn't have to be drudgery. We all get discouraged. Rest when you have to. Then do what you can. Tackle the small parts you understand. When working with your friends on the same goals, you'll have memories for life, plus the fun you'll have!

9. Help those behind you. Aren't these a part of your requirements? By teaching others you will also be gaining skills in leadership and public speaking. Believe it or not, you help yourself when you are an aid to others. You take your focus off your own problems when you help those around you with theirs. You'll make friends by being a friend.

10. Do no harm; learn to be productive. Nobody is born loving work, but work is the only method given to us to accomplish anything.

These general suggestions are to encourage the Scout to accomplish what he can, to do his best. After Scouting, apply these same principles to your education and vocation.

Happy Scouting!

Musical Scouts

WHILE MEETING WITH CHUCK WAGNER concerning Mr. Street's upcoming 83rd surprise birthday party (where we unveiled Mike Quine's Troop 826 website for him), Chuck and I happened to discuss music concerning our former Scoutmaster. Chuck said that he had been thinking about a song from Irving Berlin's "White Christmas" when remembering Mr. Street. I said that I had as well! What a coincidence. For a moment, I thought that great minds thought alike. Then he revealed the song:

We'll follow the old man wherever he wants to go
Long as he wants to go opposite to the foe
We'll stay with the old man wherever he wants to stay
Long as he stays away from the battle's fray
Because we love him, we love him
Especially when he keeps us on the ball
And we'll tell the kiddies we answered duty's call
With the grandest son of a soldier of them all!

I had also thought of the *White Christmas* movie, but the song I had in mind was different. I told him it was:

What can you do with a General (or Scoutmaster)
When he stops being a General?
Oh, what can you do with a General who retires?
Who's got a job for a General
When he stops being a General?
They all get a job but a General no one hires
It seems this country never has enjoyed
So many one- and two- and three- and four-star Generals
Unemployed.

For trivia: Did you know that the royalties for "God Bless America," a patriotic Irving Berlin hit, go straight to the Boy and Girl Scout programs even up to the present day? Pretty generous for any immigrant to part with such an amount of money to support programs he viewed as worthwhile. For a time "God Bless America" was seriously considered to become this nation's National Anthem.

The following are songs that we sang at the Thursday night Troop meetings and at the campfire on campouts. Our campfires were the highlight of the campouts. We had skits, talks, singing, ceremonies; It was generally a wrap-up time, before we had to get ready to go back home the next morning.

In a Cabin in the Woods

In a cabin in the woods
Little man by the window stood
Saw a rabbit hopping by
Knocking at his door
"Help me, help me, help", he said.
"Or the hunter will shoot me dead!"
Little rabbit come inside
Safely you'll abide

What Girls Are Made Of

Girls are made of
Greasy-grimy gopher guts
Insulated monkey meat
French-fried eyeballs,
Dirty-dirty birdy feet
And they're mixed together in
Budweiser beer.

164

Worms

Nobody likes me
Everybody hates me
I'm gonna eat some worms!
Nice big juicey worms
Slip-slop slimey worms
Fuzzy-wuzzy wuzzy wuzzy worms.
First one was easy
Second one was greasy
Third one got stuck in my throat
Choke! *Choke!*
Nice big juicy worms
Slip-slop slimey worms
Fuzzy-wuzzy wuzzy wuzzy worms!
Up comes the first one
Up comes the second one
Third one's coming *UP* soon!
Nice big juicey worms
Slip-slop slimey worms
Fuzzy-wuzzy wuzzy wuzzy worms!

Little Rabbit Foo-Foo

Little rabbit Foo-Foo,
hopping through the forest,
Scooping up the field mice,
and bopping them on the head,
And down came the good fairy, and she said,
"Little rabbit Foo-Foo,
I don't want to see you
Scooping up the field mice,
and bopping them on the head."
"I'll give you three chances,
and then I'll turn you into a goon."
But the very next day . . .
(repeat the verse)
"I'll give you two more chances,
and then I'll turn you into a goon."
But the very next day . . .
(repeat the verse)
"I'll give you one more chance,
and then I'll turn you into a goon."
But the very next day . . .
(repeat the verse)
"I gave you three chances, So now I'll
turn you into a goon."—Zap!
The moral of the story is: "Hare today;
Goon tomorrow." (spoken by all)

Six Pence

In Britain, the plural of "penny" is "pence" when referring to a quantity of money and "pennies" when referring to a number of coins. Thus a coin worth five times as much as one penny is worth five pence, but "five pennies" means five coins, each of which is a penny.

I've got six pence,
Jolly olly six pence
I've got six pence
To last me all my life!
I've got two pence to spend, and
Two pence to lend, and
Two pence to give unto my wife,
Poor wife!
No fears have I to grieve me,
No sexy little girls to dece-ee-eive me!
I'm as happy as a lark, be-lie-eve me!
When we go rolling-rolling on . . .
Rolling On! Rolling ON!
By the light of the sil-very moo-oo-oo-oon!
Happy is the day
When the staff goes away!
And we go rolling-rolling on!
I've got four pence!
Jolly olly four pence, [and so on]

Yellow Bird

The leader sings the first line, and the group sings the second line throughout the song.

A yellow bird
A yellow bird
with a yellow bill
with a yellow bill
was sitting on
was sitting on
my window sill
my window sill
I lured him in
I lured him in
with a piece of bread
with a piece of bread
and then I crushed
and then I crushed
his little head
his little head

John Jacob Jingleheimer Schmidt

John Jacob Jingleheimer Schmidt
That's my name too
Whenever I'm about
The people always shout:
"John Jacob Jingleheimer Schmidt!"
Tra-la-la-la-la-la-la . . .
(Sing the song normally, sing it a second time, then quietly
the third time, until the final line...)
"John Jacob Jingleheimer Schmidt!"

Taps

Day is done
Gone the sun
From the hills,
From the lake,
From the sky.
All is well,
Safely rest,
God is nigh

More Musical Scouts

Looking back at the end of our childhood and with the onset of adolescence, much of the fun we had was related to the Boy Scouts and Irving Troop 826. It was a bright time in our lives. I'm reminded of the lyrics from Lerner and Lowe's "Camelot," when at the end of the play King Arthur tells the young to remember his Kingdom when they reminiscence:

"Finale Ultimo (Camelot Reprise)"

ARTHUR:

Each evening, from December to December,
Before you drift to sleep upon your cot,
Think back on all the tales that you remember
of Camelot.
Ask ev'ry person if he's heard the story,
And tell it strong and clear if he has not,
That once there was a fleeting wisp of glory
called Camelot.
CHORUS:
Don't let it be forgot
That once there was a spot
For one brief shining moment that was known
as Camelot.

TROOP 826 ROLL CALL

Scoutmaster Warren Street
Assistant Scoutmaster Bob Nelson †
Committee Chairman Ray Mahaffey Sr.

Eagle Scouts

1970 Jack Rankin
1970 Duane Tarver
1971 Ray Mahaffey Jr.†
1972 Mike Quine
1978 Steve Rackley †

Our Troop

Richard Abbott
Robbie Ahlgren
Jimmy Allen
Troy Allen
Dale Alexander
John Altweis
Rickey Anderson
Floyd Andrews
Freddie Armer
Hugh Ashburn
Larry Baker
David Barnes
Jimmy Barnes
Larry Battin
David Bennett
Richard Bennett
Bobby Borah †

Chris Boyd
Greg Bridie
Joel Brockett
Ronald Brooks
Alvin Brown
Louis Brown
James Bruns
Robert Burgman
Jerry Burton
Jimmy Butterworth
Don Caffey
Clifford Cain
Monte Carrigan
James Carter
Troy Cates
Chris Chance
Charles Choate
Greg Cober
Jimmy Comer
Bobby Copeland
David Copeland
Robert Cover
Randy Cowart
Gary Cox
Fred Curtis
Mike Curtis
Billy Dahlgren
Richard Dahlgren
John Danford
Richard Danford
Robert Davis
Ronald Davis
John Deardorff

Richard Deardorff
Randy Deffenbaugh †
Jeff Dempsey
Michael DeVillez
Mark Dixon
Bruce Dorman
Rod Egger
Steven Fellows †
Jimmy Finley
John Bentley Foster
Gayland Freeman
Phillip Freeman
Mike Freestone
Dewayne Freudenrich
Greg Furr
Albert Garner
Joe George
Carl Grindstaff
Douglas Hale
Rocky Hall
Chuck Hart †
Ronnie Hargrove
Gary Hatch
Ronnie Heflin
Jimmy Higginbotham
Mike Huebner
Bob Hughs
Larry Humphrey
Eddie Jacobs
Curtis (Eddie) Jenkins
Mike Johnson
Todd Johnston

Scott Jones
Richard Jourden
James Josey
Michael Kelley
Joseph Kittner
Russell Koenig
Martin Kollhoff
Timmy Lambkin
Robert Lanter
Kenneth Luster
Mike Luster
Don Lyon
Paul Maples
Donald Martin
Billy Maus
Mike Maus
Robert Maxfield Jr.
Scott Maxwell
Charles May
Henry May
Tim McAlister
Greg McCall
Bobby McCormack
Andy McFerrin
Bart McGibboney
Gary McGregor
Ricky Metzler
Don Wesley Michael
Billy Mitchell
Lincoln Monroe
Daryl Moore
Greg Morgan
Robbie Morgan

Joey Mullican
Steve Mullican
Donnie Mullins
Ronnie Mullins
Gary Nelson
Rick Norman
Rusty Norman
Mark Null †
Tony Obennoskey
Phil Parham
James Parkman
Jerry Patterson
Randy Patton
Gene Peters
Michael Pickett
Monte Pipes
Ronny Pipes
Randall Poole
Edmund Ponikiewski †
Richard Ponikiewski
Bobby Joe Porter
Tommy Poyma
Tony Poyma
Kevin Quine †
Doug Reed †
Mike Reed
Steve Reynolds
Bill Richardson
Ronnie Riddle
David Robinson
Terry Roy
David Safran
Steve Safran

Richard Salas †
Harvey Sanders
Troy Scott
Mike Shelton
Mike Shepard
Andy Shipp
Carl Dee Smith
Joseph Shrengohst
Charles Smith
Lyle Snow
Richard Stallings
Richard Street
Rodney Street
Bob Stripling
Rodney Sumner
Gary Thetford
Jerry Thetford
Tony Thomas
Kenny Trammel
Mike Wade
Chuck Wagner
Jack Wagner
Alan Walls
Mike Walker
Ronnie Wells
Brack Whitley
John Wilkins
Neal Wilkins
Conley Williams
Monty Williams
Tommy Williams
Bryan Witty
David Yarbro

Jody Yarbro
Mike Young
Rusty Zachary
Robert Zdziarski

† Scouts who have passed away

More books by Richard J. Bennett
(Available at AMAZON.Com and KINDLE.com)

Faith and Labor: *An Examination of a Texas Public High School*

The Lovely Chocolate Mob
(available at AUDIBLE.com and itunes.com)

The Mighty Hogs of Lovely High
(also available at AUDIBLE.com and itunes.com)

Mike, the Bike, and the Great Big Fight
(a short story)

Websites

www.richardjbennett.com

www.fineartamerica.com/profiles/4-richard-bennett

86773629R00108

Made in the USA
Lexington, KY
15 April 2018